MEDICAL MALPRACTICE INSURANCE

MEDICAL MALPRACTICE INSURANCE

A Legislator's View

TARKY LOMBARDI, Jr.
New York State Senator

with **GERALD N. HOFFMAN**

SYRACUSE UNIVERSITY PRESS
1978

Library of Congress Cataloging in Publication Data

Lombardi, Tarky.
   Medical malpractice insurance.
   Includes bibliographical references and index.
    1. Insurance, Physicians' liability—United States.
I. Hoffman, Gerald N., joint author. II. Title.
[DNLM: 1. Insurance, Liability—United States.
2. Malpractice. W44 L842m]
HG8054.P5L65   368.5   78–6409
ISBN 0–8156–0128–X

Manufactured in the United States of America

To Marianne and Elizabeth

Tarky Lombardi, Jr., New York State Senator, is Chairman of the Senate Health Committee and author of New York State's 1975 Medical Malpractice Law. He served on the Governor's Special Advisory Panel on Medical Malpractice and is the author of legislation, now law, that created the designation of physician's assistant, expanded prepaid group practice and home health care, assisted voluntary ambulance services to provide professional training for emergency personnel, and assured continuity of ambulatory care in nonprofit hospitals.

Senator Lombardi is also a member of State Senate Committees on Codes, Education, Finance, and Higher Education.

A graduate of Syracuse University's Colleges of Business Administration and Law, Senator Lombardi is a partner in the law firm of Lombardi, Devorsetz, Stinziano, and Smith.

·∘][∘··

Contents

TABLES

Foreword

The medical malpractice problem, as many have slowly begun to realize, is going to be with us a while longer. Notwithstanding the fairly common belief that it erupted almost overnight, it was a long time in coming, with insurance cost and availability problems having plagued doctors and hospitals in selected states for more than twenty years. The situation had reached such menacing proportions in California by 1959 that a *Saturday Evening Post* writer was able to comment: "Unquestionably, the malpractice problem has become one of the most serious in the modern practice of medicine. Medical authorities have described it as shocking, humiliating, and dangerous. One Los Angeles hospital official stated only two years ago, 'The situation is becoming acute in many parts of the Nation, but in Los Angeles it is already intolerable.'"

Little did the author of those remarks realize how much worse things were to get two decades later, with doctors' strikes in California and elsewhere bringing health services to a virtual standstill for several weeks in many parts of the nation. What distinguished the mid-1970s malpractice crisis from earlier ones was not the fundamental nature of the problem, but simply its pervasiveness. Suddenly the public was made privy to what had theretofore been a problem affecting a tiny segment of our population, and one that appeared to be quite capable of looking out for its own interests. And while the tactics employed may have been novel (at least for the medical profession) they produced some rather dramatic results. Doctors were at last able to enlist public sympathy and support for a wide range of so-called tort reform measures and companion legislation designed to correct what were deemed to be inequities in the prosecution of medical malpractice claims.

ix

But much had occurred in the intervening years. In 1969 Senator Abraham Ribicoff's Subcommittee on Executive Reorganization had issued its massive study on medical malpractice, outlining many of the root issues. In early 1970 the American Osteopathic Association, in conjunction with the U.S. Department of Health, Education and Welfare, hosted the First National Conference on Medical Malpractice in Chicago—a conference that was to bring together for the first time all the concerned interest groups: doctors, lawyers, insurers, hospital officials, and state and federal authorities. Once again, most of the fundamental malpractice issues were raised and debated, and many valuable recommendations for change ensued. A conference in late 1970 sponsored by the Center for the Study of Democratic Institutions at Santa Barbara, California, brought together a select group of thinkers who addressed the issue of alternative medical injury compensation systems for the first time. And finally, in 1971 the Secretary of Health, Education and Welfare established the Commission on Medical Malpractice, which was to address the manifold concomitants of medical malpractice for eighteen months and whose 1973 report formed the basis for much that we know about the problem today.

The present volume picks up the thread of the malpractice issue with the events precipitating the highly publicized breakdown of the medical malpractice insurance system in 1975–76. It admirably focuses on the many interacting forces which produced the breakdown—insurance carrier solvency problems, malpractice ratemaking problems, changing public perceptions of doctors and medicine, legal system problems, and the like. It also gives the reader a perspective he or she may be less aware of, that of the dedicated legislator earnestly seeking solutions to a very complex problem fraught with emotional overtones and more than its share of vested-interest rhetoric. As Chairman of the New York State Senate Health Committee, as well as a member of the Governor's Special Advisory Panel on Medical Malpractice, Senator Lombardi became intimately familiar with the many complex and controversial issues surrounding medical malpractice, and his first-hand account of the up-front and behind-the-scenes maneuvering while this issue was being debated in New York is a valuable contribution to the literature on this subject.

As we now know, the unprecedented work stoppages by doctors in California, New York, and several other states in 1975 prompted a frenzy of legislative activity at the state level. Hundreds

of bills, mostly concerned with the availability of insurance and rec-
ommending changes in the tort system, were introduced in state-
houses all over the nation. Malpractice study commissions were
established in just about every state in the union, and many have already reported their findings to their respective legislatures.
Whether the resultant legislation will prove helpful in the long run
remains to be seen. But even a casual survey of the rash of malpractice reforms enacted to date shows the inordinate attention devoted
to insurance and legal system concomitants compared to recommended improvements in health system quality controls, injury prevention, and the like. It is as though the legislatures, in their
headlong rush to "get something on the books," ignored the indis-
putable precipitating cause of the entire problem—medical injury—
preferring instead to deal with better-understood and more manage-
able issues. A disappointing number of the enacted tort reform laws
simply make it harder for malpractice victims to assert or prosecute
their claims, or arbitrarily limit the amounts they may recover—a
result long sought by malpractice insurers, but with little success. It
is clear that they, with the help of their health care policyholders,
were able to seize upon the malpractice "crisis" as a means of
enlisting public support for a host of reform measures designed to
serve their own—rather than the public's—best interests. "A
crisis," as political scientist Paul Starr has noted, "can be a truly
marvelous mechanism for the withdrawal or suspension of established rights, and the acquisition and legitimation of new privileges." When dealing with issues as complex and controversial as
the malpractice problem, the public seldom has a clear conception
of what its interests are, and it may be a while before some balance
is restored to the situation.

To be sure, malpractice insurance is now generally available
to doctors and hospitals, albeit at higher rates than in the past. But
all the factors which created the crisis of 1975–76 in the first place
remain essentially unchanged. The present situation can best be described as a temporary lull, a hiatus in the long series of cyclical
crises that have characterized the malpractice phenomenon. Senator Lombardi thinks that most of the new malpractice legislation is
little more than "a finger in the dike or band aid, when major surgery is required." I believe he is absolutely right on this point. Problems with our malpractice claims system are merely symptomatic of
deeper problems. How we handle malpractice claims is only a part
of the much broader problem of how to compensate all accidental

injury—an issue that our country has not yet addressed in any comprehensive fashion.

Perhaps our greatest need is to re-think the malpractice problem from a broader vantage point. If malpractice claims are attributable primarily to maloccurrences in the treatment process, should we not be devoting more attention to the development of health system quality controls that will reduce their frequency? Is it possible to build into the present (fault-based) malpractice system a better assortment of rewards and sanctions so that substandard practices are prevented more effectively while, at the same time, injured patients are not forced to wait years before receiving just compensation? In the final analysis, why even single out victims of medical malpractice (or those who cause their injuries) for special treatment? Are the needs of malpractice victims any different than those of victims of auto accidents, victims of criminal assaults, or victims of harmful defective products? Should our entire focus not be changed—from an overriding concern for guaranteeing malpractice insurance to doctors and hospitals to guaranteeing prompt rehabilitation and prompt compensation to all injured patients?

The answers to questions of this sort would go a long way toward solving the very serious problem of injury reparations in this country, of which malpractice claims are only a minute part. In the meantime, we have little choice but to direct our best efforts toward improving the existing system—flawed though it may be—in the hope of making it more responsive to the needs of all our citizens. Knowing how we got where we are is an important part of that process, and the present volume sheds new light on many issues not previously discussed. It should give those in a position to bring about change a better understanding of the limitations of the present system and the direction in which it is headed.

Washington, D.C.   Eli P. Bernzweig, J.D.
Spring 1978   *Federal Executive Fellow*
                                                  The Brookings Institution,
                                       and Former Executive Director,
                                          HEW Secretary's Commission
                                              on Medical Malpractice

·⊃⫚⊂·

Acknowledgments

There are thousands of unsung people at all levels of government in this country who rarely receive recognition for the services they perform on behalf of their fellow human beings. Unfortunately the attention given to public servants usually goes to those who have fallen short of the standards expected of those in public office and public employment.

In particular, I would like to acknowledge the staff members of the New York State Legislature and various state departments and agencies who worked with the Senate Health Committee and me on the problems of medical malpractice. Harriet Morse, director of the Committee, and Edward Grogan, Esquire, counsel to the Committee, as always, ably assisted the chairman as they have done on so many other issues in the health field.

Legislators, department heads, attorneys, insurance experts, and health care providers are among those in New York State and across the nation who have contributed greatly not only to our deliberations on medical malpractice but also to the preparation of this text.

A special word of appreciation goes to Eli P. Bernzweig, former staff director of the U.S. Secretary of Health, Education and Welfare's Commission on Medical Malpractice, who is so generous in offering his expertise to any efforts to seek a better system which is more efficient and effective in disposing of malpractice claims and which is equitable for patients, their families, and health care providers.

Finally, I would like to thank Gerald N. Hoffman, my executive assistant and associate for thirteen years, who collaborated with me on this project.

Syracuse, New York   *Tarky Lombardi, Jr.*
Spring 1978

·∘]Ϳ·

Introduction

M EDICAL MALPRACTICE, a very complex subject which was formerly
the domain of insurance companies, attorneys, physicians,
and a relatively small group of claimants, suddenly emerged as a
major issue in the mid-1970s.

Insurance premiums for doctors and hospitals had been skyrocketing for many years, but public attention was not focused on
this problem until a number of insurance carriers withdrew from
the medical malpractice market. Threatened by loss of insurance
coverage or coverage at rates they believed to be exorbitant, health
care providers and health care facilities took their case to the general public and their elected state legislators.

Talk of possible doctors' strikes and work slowdowns by
medical personnel, which became a reality in some states, served to
raise the issue to crisis proportions in the eyes of the public and
most state legislators.

Not all legislators, however, were willing to accept as a fact
that medical malpractice was a genuine crisis and was not merely a
situation which had been created by insurance companies or by doctors, and was not another "ripoff" of the American public.

The definition of the term "medical malpractice" itself became part of the controversy surrounding the issue, particularly in
the ranks of the medical profession. Doctors for the most part
thought that attorneys and the courts had turned medical malpractice into some sort of a compensation system for patients with unfavorable outcomes from medical treatment, as opposed to damages
suffered as a result of malpractice.

For purposes of this book, medical malpractice as defined in
Black's Law Dictionary, means "generally professional misconduct

toward a patient which is considered reprehensible either because immoral in itself or because contrary to law or expressly forbidden by law, and in a more specific sense it means bad, wrong, or injudicious treatment of a patient, professionally, and in respect to the particular disease or injury resulting in injury, unnecessary suffering or death to the patient, disregard of established rules or principles, neglect of a malicious or criminal intent."

In coming to grips with the malpractice issue, legislators had to weave their way through a maze of related topics such as the intricate insurance aspects, disciplining of doctors, and a multitude of legal considerations related to a claimant's right to sue and to recover for acts of medical malpractice.

As Chairman of the New York State Senate Health Committee, and as a member of the Governor's Special Advisory Panel on Medical Malpractice, I devoted nearly two full years of almost constant work on this issue. This book, which originally started as a chronicle of my involvement and that of my staff with this subject, is offered in the hope that it will generate better understanding not only of the malpractice problem but of the tremendous difficulty in legislating effective solutions. The book can also provide an example of how the legislative process tackles a controversial and complex issue.

The legislator, in effect, becomes both judge and jury. He or she is often confronted with conflicting stories and arguments from lobbyists, representatives of special interest groups, and individual citizens. After weighing the evidence, the legislator must make a decision and cast a vote whether it is in committee or on the floor of the legislature.

What follows is an account of the malpractice issue as seen through the eyes of one state legislator, who, although an attorney, has never been involved in malpractice litigation and who tackled the issue with no preconceived biases. In addressing the medical malpractice problem, it has been my intention to act not in the interests of doctors, insurance carriers, hospitals, or attorneys, but rather to assist patients and their families by assuring the continued availability of health care services.

As a legislator I have reached certain conclusions and advocate a number of steps to protect the patient and to preserve the health care delivery system as we know it. However, particular emphasis has been placed on presenting all sides of this issue fairly.

This accounts for numerous long passages of quoted material expressing differing viewpoints.

Chapter 1 considers the insurance aspects of malpractice. Chapter 2 presents the views of doctors, Chapter 3 the concerns of hospitals, and Chapter 4 the perspective of trial lawyers. Chapter 5 centers on medical discipline. Chapter 6 reviews the work of the U.S. Secretary of Health, Education and Welfare's Commission on Medical Malpractice and includes comments of the commissioners on subsequent events. Chapter 7 is a case study of the issue in New York State and the legislative response in that state. Chapter 8 covers legislative activity and the malpractice issue in other states and other countries, and Chapter 9 offers conclusions and recommendations for future legislative action concerning medical malpractice.

The adversary roles of insurance companies, doctors, and attorneys who accused the others of being the culprits and the causes for the problem have made it difficult for legislators and the general public to fully understand the issue and to determine what should be done about it, since the issue is still far from being resolved.

In retrospect, the medical malpractice issue has forced many of us to take a hard and sometimes painful look at the time-honored professions of law and medicine and to ask ourselves how they might better cope with and meet the needs of today's society.

MEDICAL MALPRACTICE INSURANCE

An Unprofitable Risk?

W HEN LAYMEN AND LEGISLATORS begin to consider the medical malpractice issue, they are in most instances ill-equipped to cope
with the insurance aspects which are at the heart of the problem.
Medical malpractice would not have surfaced as a concern of state
legislators and the public had doctors and hospitals not had difficulties in obtaining insurance coverage.

To most of us, insurance is a perplexing and puzzling area.
The language of insurance includes many terms which are foreign to
our ears and our eyes. Despite the fact that insurance companies
pay out billions of dollars in claims, they do not receive a favorable
rating from the average citizen, who has an image of the companies
as cold, impersonal entities that use his premium money to reap
huge profits. Form letters that reject claims help create a negative
attitude for the general public.

An insurance agent who has spent more than twenty years in
the field stated that one well-known company's policy is to reject all
claims initially. "This procedure," the agent said, "eliminates 25
percent of the claims."

Given such ideas about insurance and practices of insurance
companies, it was no wonder that the American public was skeptical
when talk began about a medical malpractice insurance crisis. Although malpractice premiums countrywide for doctors and hospitals
rose from $61 million in 1960 to $1 billion in 1975, it was difficult to
convince legislators and taxpayers that insurance companies were
not profiting from malpractice.

Senator Edward M. Kennedy said: "It is all too reminiscent of
what happened to gas and oil prices during the Arab embargo."[1]
Skeptics who believed that oil companies had taken advantage of the

embargo to raise their prices had similar concerns about the malpractice crisis and insurance companies. Despite serious misgivings about the industry's response to the medical malpractice issue, the author in all fairness must state that there is little evidence to substantiate the point of view that the crisis was contrived for the benefit of the insurance company. Lester Rawls, the highly respected insurance commissioner of the State of Oregon and chairman of the Committee on Malpractice of the National Association of Insurance Commissioners, concurred. Rawls said: "This is not a fantasy.... It is real.... These people are telling the truth. The companies—they are greedy enough that if there was a buck to be made, they would be in there."[2]

Malpractice is no longer a profitable line of insurance, according to many sources. In 1975, Wesley J. Kinder, insurance commissioner of the State of California, said: "We cannot find any insurer that has made a profit on this line in California. We cannot find any proposed rate to be excessive."[3]

The California experience is indicative of national trends concerning medical malpractice insurance. Andrew Kalmykow, counsel for the American Insurance Association, said: "The most recent figures issued by the Insurance Services Office, the national statistical and rating agency for the insurance industry, indicate that losses, that is, payouts to claimants and defense costs, alone will exceed 150 per cent of total premiums received. In other words, companies writing this business will have to pay out 50 per cent more in losses than they received in premiums. In addition, of course, insurance companies incurred administrative and other necessary expenses."[4]

Lawrence O. Monin, first deputy superintendent of insurance in New York State, told two state legislative committees that "medical malpractice insurance is an extremely risky form of insurance, and over the past few years it has consistently been unprofitable. It has been unprofitable even though this period has also been marked by rapid and substantial medical malpractice rate increases." Monin noted that Employers Insurance of Wausau suffered a net loss of $120 million as a result of its coverage of the approximately 23,000 members of the New York State Medical Society from 1949 to 1972.[5]

James H. Durkin, actuary for the New York State Medical Society, commented: "It is not justified to contend that historical rate increases were due to insurance company profiteering. My actuarial analysis convinces me that the long-time insurer on this program made money in the 1950s, but lost money in the 1960s; and that rates for that carrier in 1971, 1972, and 1973 were adequate, but not excessive."[6]

Argonaut Insurance Company of California succeeded Employers as the carrier for the New York State Medical Society in July 1974. Since the company became a major focal point of the malpractice crisis in New York and many states, a review of the Argonaut experience is not only informative but also sets the background for more detailed discussion of malpractice insurance.

Prior to the "crisis," Argonaut was recognized as one of the most dynamic, rapidly growing workmen's compensation carriers in the country, and from an operational standpoint it was regarded as conservative and well-managed. Argonaut, which had been taken over by the conglomerate Teledyne, Inc., in 1969, first wrote malpractice coverage for a state hospital association in the Midwest. The company placed heavy emphasis on injury prevention, and its subsequent experience with the malpractice policyholders made it possible to reward them with a dividend. Word of Argonaut's initial success in the malpractice field spread quickly and led to a number of statewide programs involving substantial premiums for the carrier.

The plunge into the malpractice market by Argonaut came at a time when other carriers, concerned about rising claims, settlements, and awards, were cooling off on medical malpractice business. It should be pointed out that Argonaut went into some of the states where warning signals were most noticeable—California, Florida, Massachusetts, Pennsylvania, and New York.

Initially, Teledyne was so pleased with Argonaut and its new business that the parent company pumped money into its subsidiary to increase its surplus. This transfer of funds made it possible for Argonaut to write even more malpractice coverage (all state insurance departments require a company to have an adequate premium surplus ratio, generally 2 to 1 or one dollar in the bank for every two dollars of premiums the company collects as protection against a "bad run").

Favorable conditions in the stock market and good fortunes for the insurance industry as a whole coincided with Argonaut's entrance into the malpractice field. Insurance officials concede that 1972 was perhaps the best year the industry has ever had.

The first inkling of any problems with Argonaut came in 1974 when the stock market started to plummet and malpractice losses headed upward. Teledyne's top management began to ask questions of Argonaut in 1973, but the answers apparently satisfied the parent company until July 1974 when losses and claims frequency began to steamroll. Within a few months, the chairman of the board and the president of Argonaut were fired, and Harry Singleton, chairman of the board of Teledyne, assumed direct personal control of Argonaut's total operations.

Singleton and his key personnel soon learned that their subsidiary was top heavy in medical malpractice business and that existing premiums were not realistic. In many states Argonaut apparently had purposely set its premiums low in order to gain the new business. The company had counted on investment income to more than offset the low premiums.

Some industry observers trace Argonaut's troubles to the death of the company's president, Jerry Taheny, shortly after Teledyne purchased Argonaut. Others claim that the company entered the medical malpractice field with little knowledge of medical malpractice, particularly premium pricing.

Lawrence C. Baker, Jr., former first deputy commissioner of the California State Insurance Department, joined Argonaut in January 1975 and was elevated to the post of president in April 1975. Baker sought to dispel any notion that the company was in bad financial shape. As of June 1975, he reported that Argonaut had assets of $582 million and a net worth of $16,291,000. He also stated that the company had a modest operating profit in the second quarter of 1975. Baker said Argonaut's underwriting loss for 1974 in hospital liability was $35 million and in medical malpractice the loss was approximately $47 million.[7]

Many public officials trying to assess Argonaut's activities in the malpractice field were surprised and disturbed to find that Argonaut had paid Teledyne a $10.5 million dividend in 1974. They were also at a loss to fully explain how Argonaut's surplus, reportedly $128 million in 1973, dipped to $28 million a year later.[8]

Baker told Florida authorities that $50 million of the $100 million decline was a result of increases in loss reserves. Adding in the $10.5 million dividend paid to Teledyne, $39.5 million was still unaccounted for in Argonaut's explanation of its financial condition.

Argonaut's proposed premium increases, announced in late 1974 and early 1975, triggered a chain reaction throughout the health care industry. Argonaut's troubles and the subsequent malpractice crisis did not catch everyone by surprise. As one insurance executive commented, it was "a sudden flare of a fire that was burning for some time."

Other insurance industry responses were along the lines of "if Argonaut is having trouble, let's prepare for the worst." Many carriers asked themselves: "Should we stay in the business?" Their answer was: "Yes, if we price it properly."

Ronald E. Ferguson, vice-president of General Reinsurance Corporation, in a letter to Senator Edward Kennedy, said: "We feel that the increases posted in 1974 and 1975 represent a wrenching period of catch-up necessitated in some cases by overly optimistic assumptions used in the ratemaking process prior to 1974, recalcitrant regulators in other cases, and judicial changes."[9]

Unfortunately, from the companies' standpoint, doctors and hospitals in many states rebelled and would not accept large premium increases. Since the carriers were unable to get the price they felt necessary to continue insuring the malpractice risk, many companies put policyholders on notice that they were withdrawing from the malpractice market, which was only a small part of their underwriting portfolio.

In 1975 malpractice premiums represented only 2.3 percent of the total property/liability business,[10] and a smaller part of the whole insurance industry. For example, in 1973 Michigan doctors paid $11 million in malpractice premiums while auto insurance premiums for the same state were $900 million.[11] There have never been more than fifty companies in the malpractice field; fifteen to twenty of them write 75 to 80 percent of the business.[12]

A word picture of the medical malpractice insurance scene in an insurance company portrayed "the president of the company at the steering wheel of an automobile, the vice-president of marketing with both feet on the accelerator, the vice-president of underwriting with both feet on the brakes, and the actuary looking out the back window and calling out directions."[13]

Warren Cooper, then vice-president and actuary for Chubb & Son, Inc., said the main reason for the "availability crunch" was the inability as insurance people to project the price that we really feel should be charged for this line of business, for in our economic scheme, the business really operates effectively only if they can accurately predict what they should charge.[14]

While doctors and others were critical about the role of insurance companies in the so-called crisis, Cooper criticized the physician's lack of knowledge about insurance. "Doctors forget what insurance is—a pooling of risk. If we could predict their losses, we would advise them to set aside their own money."[15]

In their report to the California Legislature Booz, Allen Consulting Actuaries of California claimed that "the current malpractice crisis has been caused in part by poor pricing by the insurance industry."[16]

Raymond H. Bohl, vice-president for the special accounts division of Employers Insurance of Wausau, pinpointed what most experts cite as the chief culprit in malpractice insurance: "In no other insurable area is there so great a lag between the date of the act or omission for which claim is made and the date of its final disposition."[17] This time lag is called the "tail" of malpractice coverage.

Reports from the State of California Insurance Department (Tables 1 and 2) indicate that, of the cases studied, all of the claims reported for a given policy year did not surface until twelve years later. Twenty-one years elapsed before all payments were made.[18] This time lag or "tail" is costly and troublesome to insurance companies, victims, and policyholders. This is not the situation with other lines of coverage.

Maturity of medical malpractice claims is an average of 123 months, or nearly double that of automobile insurance, 63 months, and considerably longer than that for products liability, which is 75 months. The industry's rule of thumb, or as it is called, the loss development factor, used to multiply figures from the first evaluations to projected final costs at maturity, is 3.019 for malpractice, compared with 1.915 for products liability and 1.667 for auto insurance.[19]

Another feature separating medical malpractice insurance from other lines is the ability of doctors to approve or disapprove the carrier's recommendation to settle a claim. The Industry Advisory Committee to the Professional Liability Subcommittee of the National Association of Insurance Commissioners said: "The removal of the consent clause found in many medical malpractice policies will probably help to make claims handling more efficient. This clause is unique to professional liability policies and its absence in other liability contracts has induced more prompt reparation to the injured party."[20] Representatives of insurance companies, however,

Table 1

MEDICAL MALPRACTICE NUMBER OF CLAIMS REPORTED

Months from Beginning of Policy Year	Number of Claims Reported (%)	Months from Beginning of Policy Year	Number of Claims Reported (%)
24	38	78	92
30	55	84	93
36	67	90	94
42	74	96	95
48	79	102	95
54	83	108	96
60	86	120	98
66	89	132	99
72	91	144	100

Source: Exhibit A, Memorandum from Wesley J. Kinder, Insurance Commissioner, to Donald E. Burns, Secretary, Business and Transportation Agency, State of California, Sacramento, California, June 2, 1975.

Table 2

MEDICAL MALPRACTICE CLAIMS PAID

Months from Beginning of Policy Year	Dollars Paid as a Percentage of Ultimate (%)	Months from Beginning of Policy Year	Dollars Paid as a Percentage of Ultimate (%)
24	2.5	144	95.2
36	7.5	156	96.6
48	17.2	168	97.8
60	32.7	180	98.3
72	52.4	192	98.5
84	70.6	204	98.7
96	81.3	216	99.1
108	87.0	228	99.4
120	91.3	240	99.5
132	94.1	252	100.0

Source: Exhibit B, Memorandum from Wesley J. Kinder, Insurance Commissioner, to Donald E. Burns, Secretary, Business and Transportation Agency, State of California, Sacramento, California, June 2, 1975.

Table 3

DEVELOPMENT OF INCURRED LOSSES
Physicians' and Surgeons' Professional Liability Insurance

Policy Year Ending 12/31/66

Total Limits Premium: $13,544,524

Evaluation Date	Total Limits Incurred Losses*	Estimated Paid Losses
3/31/67	$ 5,559,547	$ 1,000,000
3/31/68	11,634,040	
3/31/69	16,110,052	
3/31/70	17,703,591	
3/31/71	18,185,503	
3/31/72	19,344,529	
3/31/73	19,511,506	
3/31/74	20,174,516	18,200,000
3/31/75	20,200,000	18,600,000

*Includes all loss adjustment expenses.

Source: ISO (Insurance Services Office), New York City, 1975; updated by letter to New York State Senate Health Committee, July 1977.

do not necessarily view the consent clause as a significant factor in resolving the malpractice problem.

Establishing a ceiling on awards which later was enacted in some states is more helpful in trying to predict future losses with some degree of certainty.

Warren Cooper said the advent of awards of $1 million and more increased the inability of insurance personnel to predict with any degree of accuracy what today's premiums should be to finance tomorrow's losses.[21] Cooper and other insurance company executives referred to Table 3, prepared by the Insurance Services Office, which charts the development of incurred losses for the policy year 1966 to back up their argument. During that year malpractice premiums in the amount of $13,544,524 were collected in this country. As of March 31, 1975, estimated paid losses were set at $20,400,000, which bolsters the contention that premiums and reserves, at least for the year 1966, were not sufficient to pay for ultimate losses. Actually paid losses were $18.6 million. "Once policyholder-supplied

Table 4

POLICY YEAR 1965
CLAIMS PAYMENT BY YEAR

	Yearly Payout	Cumulative Payout	
Premiums earned in 1965			$4,850,000
Payouts during years:			
1966	$ 92,000	$ 92,000	
1967	243,000	335,000	
1968	483,000	818,000	
1969	817,000	1,635,000	
1970	1,265,000	2,900,000	
1971	1,053,000	3,953,000	
1972	1,364,000	5,317,000	
1973	1,243,000	6,551,000	
1974	766,000	7,327,000	
End of policy year to 12/31/74	628,000	7,955,000	7,955,000
Payout in excess of premium earned			$3,105,000

Source: Table 2, Interim Report, Joint Legislative Audit Committee, Office of the Auditor General, California Legislature, September 10, 1975, p. 13.

funds have been used up, i.e., used to pay claims, the loss reserves must still be maintained, and they are, but out of company surplus."[22]

Table 4 traces the development of claims paid in the State of California for the policy year 1965. Premiums collected in the year 1965 amounted to $4,850,000. Paid claims based on 1965 cases have far exceeded that amount. Payouts or losses on the 1965 premiums had reached $7,955,000 by the end of 1974.

Table 5 shows that, from 1960 to 1974, $262 million in malpractice premiums were collected in California while the companies paid out only $115 million. On the surface it would appear that the carriers reaped a large profit. This does not take into account the money that ultimately will be paid out on claims for policies written during those years. It is estimated that companies will in the long run pay out $183 million more than they collected.[23] (Tables showing the losses of all carriers in the State of California in recent years are in Appendix A.)

Table 5

Summary of Premiums Earned For Physician Malpractice Insurance Compared to Actual Claims Paid by Insurance Companies Reviewed 1960 through 1974

Year	Doctors Insured	Premiums Earned	Claims Paid For the Year	Under (Over) Premiums Earned	Claims Paid During the Year*	Under (Over) Premiums Earned
1960	3,870	$ 1,731,000	$ 4,591,000	$ 140,000	$ 2,000	$ 1,729,000
1961	3,830	1,711,000	1,277,000	434,000	1,000	1,710,000
1962	3,810	1,746,000	1,689,000	58,000	1,000	1,746,000
1963	9,990	3,942,000	4,942,000	(1,000,000)	4,000	3,938,000
1964	10,990	4,474,000	6,105,000	(1,631,000)	20,000	4,454,000
1965	11,660	4,850,000	7,955,000	(3,105,000)	372,000	4,478,000
1966	12,950	6,035,000	10,980,000	(4,945,000)	982,000	5,052,000
1967	15,220	8,570,000	14,294,000	(5,724,000)	1,567,000	7,003,000
1968	17,420	13,914,000	14,633,000	(719,000)	3,313,000	10,601,000
1969	18,160	24,810,000	16,128,000	8,681,000	3,124,000	21,686,000
1970	16,090	29,937,000	13,613,000	16,324,000	5,568,000	24,370,000
1971	18,030	35,607,000	13,609,000	21,998,000	12,274,000	23,333,000
1972	18,890	36,442,000	6,185,000	30,257,000	19,608,000	16,834,000
1973	19,430	40,623,000	1,239,000	39,383,000	29,805,000	10,817,000
1974	18,330	47,642,000	423,000	47,220,000	38,022,000	9,620,000
TOTAL	198,670	$262,034,000	$114,663,000	$147,371,000	$114,663,000	$147,371,000

*None of the claims paid related to malpractice insurance written for years prior to 1960.

Source: Table 1, Interim Report, Joint Legislative Audit Committee, Office of the Auditor General, California Legislature, September 10, 1975, p. 12.

tual rate of return realized by the insurance industry for 1971–73, ... and giving recognition to the fact that collected premiums consistently have been insufficient to cover losses and expenses in this line of insurance," the investment income on loss reserves produces an average return as a percentage of earned income of 2.88 percent before federal income taxes and 2.50 percent after federal income taxes.[26]

The answers to the Kennedy questionnaire highlight one of the great difficulties facing those trying to cope with the malpractice problem. Before the end of 1975, there was a woeful lack of statistical data on the whole subject of malpractice.

Mark C. Kendall, at a conference on "The Economics of Medical Malpractice" in 1976, explained the insurance industry rationale for the lack of statistics on medical malpractice. Kendall said:

> An insurer would make the rational decision that if he writes medical malpractice insurance it is not worth the effort to collect, maintain, and analyze a large volume of medical malpractice insurance data. Resources for this data-collection effort would be better devoted to automobile insurance, which accounted for nearly 20 percent of his property and liability premium volume. Also the growth of automobile losses during the 60s would reinforce the insurer's decision.[27]

Insurance companies, state insurance commissioners, and the medical profession all share the blame for this lack of statistics. Insurance companies for years claimed that they had the figures, state insurance departments said they could get the statistics any time they needed them, and doctors objected to the collection of the malpractice information because they wanted to preserve the confidentiality of the names of physicians involved in malpractice claims.

The need to compile accurate statistical information was one of the major recommendations of the Report of the Secretary of Health, Education and Welfare's Commission on Medical Malpractice, released in January 1973. Not until the malpractice problem reached the crisis stage in early 1975 did industry and state insurance departments take steps to assemble this information on a systematic and uniform basis.

The National Association of Insurance Commissioners and the American Insurance Association, in conjunction with the industry's advisory committee for the NAIC Subcommittee on Professional Liability, worked in concert on this important effort. (See

Appendix B for summary of the All-Industry Committee report on a study of claims closed in 1974.)

The lack of statistics has helped arouse suspicion on a number of topics related to the malpractice problem. The amount of money that goes to claimants and a breakdown of where the malpractice premium dollar goes have been the subject of much debate.

Table 7 lists the insurance industry's breakdown of the premium dollar, based on rates filed by ISO (Insurance Services Office) in 1975. It is estimated that $.153 goes to the plaintiff's attorney and $.305 goes to the claimant.[28]

The California Auditor General reports that, of the closed claims studied in that state, claimants received $64 million or about 56 percent of the total claims costs. Forty percent, or $46.3 million, went for attorneys' fees, with plaintiffs' lawyers receiving 27.5 percent and defense attorneys 12.5 percent.[29]

Another topic of dispute is the reinsurance of the malpractice risk. A shortage of reinsurance was a matter of concern to Argonaut and a number of other companies. Warren Cooper said: "Smaller companies, particularly, who are dependent upon reinsurers have found extensive problems in buying reinsurance. The secondary market has receded along with the primary market. We understand that there are very few calls at Lloyds now who are willing to provide coverage to the primary American market."[30]

Reinsurance is the insurance procedure whereby the carrier, thinking it is unsound to carry the whole risk by itself, seeks out others who will pick up some of the risk. Argonaut apparently was unable to find enough reinsurers in California and New York.

Reinsurers brush off any attempt to attribute the current malpractice problems to a reinsurance shortage. One reinsurer who wished to remain anonymous commented: "Considering that reinsurers write only 8 to 9 percent of the total volume, it becomes fairly obvious that an 8 percent tail does not wag a 92 percent dog."

Reinsurance may not be a major factor in the medical malpractice picture, but others, including stock market losses and the increase in claims and awards, have affected some insurance companies. According to the Auditor General of the State of California, "our preliminary evaluation of seven malpractice insurance carriers in California indicates their financial condition has undergone serious erosion over the last five years and they currently face insolvency." The California Insurance Commissioner removed two companies from the insurance market due to insolvency. A third

Table 7

WHERE DOES THE PREMIUM DOLLAR GO?

		Portion of Premium Dollar
Total Production Cost Allowance		$ .150	
Commission and Brokerage	.120		
Other Acquisition	.030		
General Expenses		.075*	
Taxes, Licenses, and Fees		.029	
Underwriting Profit and Contingencies		.050	
Total Service and Overhead			.304
Unallocated Loss Adjustment Expenses		.069	
Allocated Loss Adjustment Expenses		.169	
Total Provision for Defense Costs			.238	
Pure Loss		.458†	
Expected Loss and Loss Adjustment Expense			.696
Total			1.000

*This item includes both general administrative expenses and boards and bureaus; a separation between those provisions is unavailable.

†A further breakdown between plaintiff's attorney's fees and benefits to the claimant is not available from insurance statistical data. However, assuming the commonly quoted estimate of one-third of the settlement as the fee for the plaintiff's attorney, then $.153 would go to the attorney and $.305 to the claimant.

Source: Answers of American Insurance Association and American Mutual Insurance Alliance to questionnaire of Senator Edward M. Kennedy, Chairman, Senate Health Subcommittee concerning medical malpractice insurance in the United States, Question 14, sheet 1, July 17, 1975, letter to Senator Kennedy, Washington, D.C.

company was restricted from writing high-risk lines of insurance such as physicians' malpractice insurance.[31]

    Underwriting and stock market losses are listed as the main factors in the downgrading of 24 percent of the nation's 1,000 liability companies by A.B. Best Company, the primary rating service for the liability insurance industry. "This was the largest number of reduced ratings in the liability insurance industry since the Depression era."[32]

The insurance industry's losses in the malpractice field, it must be remembered, are reduced considerably when one takes into account the fact that companies can recoup some of these losses in computing their taxes. In California, for example, it is estimated that tax benefits would reduce losses 48 percent from $400 million to $208 million.[33]

Despite the meteoric rise in the number of claims and amount of settlement and awards, insurers do not believe that the quality of health care has declined. In testimony at a public hearing in New York State, Raymond Bohl, of Employers Insurance of Wausau, defended doctors. Bohl said:

> Doctors are not making more mistakes, or, in any way, relaxing the quality of patient care. On the contrary, prevailing standards for the practice of medicine have never been higher than they are today, or levels of medical knowledge so high. You may well ask: If acts of malpractice are decreasing in number, how can the number of successful claims for malpractice continue to multiply. It is because the public is no longer satisfied with medical excellence. People are being taught by our courts, lawyers, and juries to expect perfection. Doctors are better than ever before. But they aren't perfect.[34]

David W. Wilson, assistant vice-president of the Medical Protective Company, successor to the country's first professional liability company, in a presentation in 1975 to a Special Committee on Medical Malpractice of the Kansas Legislature, supported Bohl and other defenders of the medical profession. Wilson said: "We find, for example, that while the majority of malpractice claims involved real injuries, most of these injuries are not the result of medical malpractice—either as to causal relationships or a failure to meet the standard of care. Further, the injury most often is not the triggering factor. The patient's dissatisfaction may be the fee, a snippy nurse, a doctor's cold and impersonal attitude, misunderstood directions, or less-than-perfect results."[35]

Thomas F. Sheehan, president of GAT Insurance Company of Chicago, emphasized that "malpractice claims against doctors are not a new phenomenon. The first case in the United States was reported in 1794. The plaintiff was awarded damages for the death of his wife because of the doctor's negligence in performing surgery."[36]

In a society that is now quick to sue, doctors and hospitals are among those who have become easy targets for legal suits.

To Rawls, the total tort system is philosophically correct but it has to be tinkered with or else it will go bankrupt. He said: "If a lawyer gets a judgment [in a medical malpractice case] and there is no money for the award, the judgment is just a piece of paper."[37]

Bernzweig is concerned about what he called a "perversion of the insurance indemnity system. He said:

> We are finding not only rising numbers of claims, but in rising numbers of cases awards being made where the negligence is, at best, rather tenuous, and certainly the thing that really decided the issue is whether or not the widow and three children sitting in the front row are ever going to have some form of compensation to make up for the loss of the loved one. . . . The jury simply says we don't care about law, we don't care about rules of negligence, that is stuff the lawyers fool around with, we are interested in doing justice for that lady in the front row and that is what has happened in the medical malpractice area.[38]

Since the malpractice issue gained prominence, the effectiveness of state insurance departments as regulators over the insurance industry has been questioned. It is debated that some insurance departments do not have adequate personnel to evaluate the reams of paper that carriers are required to submit to them each year. In other instances it is argued that personnel is sufficient, but is not used properly.

Benjamin R. Schenck, former superintendent of insurance in New York State, said in 1977 that "regulators should not have much to do with pricing. Hopefully competition will serve to keep prices at the lowest possible level."[39] He felt in 1975 that insurance departments did not have the same knowledge about medical malpractice as they have about auto insurance.[40] It is unfortunate that Schenck and others did not see the need for this information earlier.

Looking back, he said in 1977, he believed that prices for medical malpractice coverage were too low. It would have been impractical, he added, and certainly unpopular for any state insurance department to announce publicly that it was not approving rates because they were too low. Schenck said that legislators added to the malpractice crisis. "They were protesting that the premiums for doctors and hospitals were too high."[41]

Schenck thinks we will see a time when insurance companies will want to write medical malpractice policies again. As of 1977 carriers were reluctant to return to the malpractice market en masse under present conditions. Instead the industry presents a united stand in favor of significant changes in tort law which it sees as necessary before insurance companies would look upon malpractice as a line worth pursuing once again.

Many observers outside the industry may not contest the point that malpractice is unprofitable, but they are convinced that the picture is not as bleak as the carriers paint it. There are those who believe that insurance companies took advantage of Argonaut's problems and subsequent events to beat a hasty retreat from medical malpractice and leave the matter of continued coverage to public officials.

Although malpractice has become a losing proposition, some maintain that insurers have an obligation to society to provide continued coverage to doctors and hospitals.

State legislatures, by creating joint underwriting associations, in effect have said to insurance companies: "If you want to continue to write coverage in other lines in our state, you must underwrite part of the cost of providing malpractice policies to practitioners and medical facilities."

St. Paul Fire and Marine Insurance Company is one of a few firms that has remained in the malpractice business. In an attempt to reduce its risk and to permit actuaries a greater degree of certainty regarding future losses, St. Paul has instituted its claims-made policies. Under the occurrence form of malpractice insurance, the company stated it "has been underestimating the rate levels necessary to cover claims cost. The result: a $55,510,000 deficit during the five-year period 1970–1974 on medical liability business. Most of this underwriting loss—$43,491,000—came from physicians' and surgeons' business. Much of the remainder was on hospital liability."[42]

With claims-made coverage, the carrier assumes liability only for claims that are reported during the year that the policy is in effect. On a claims-occurred basis, liability is assumed by the carriers for events during the policy year regardless of when they are reported. The claims-made policy is a means of cutting the "tail" of malpractice insurance. It is estimated that in the first year a doctor would pay 40 percent of what he or she would pay under claims occurred, but, by the fifth year, the doctor would be paying the same as for a claims-occurred policy.

In 1975 other carriers maintained that claims-made was not

responsive to the problem, but simply a delaying tactic. By 1977, Warren Cooper, an industry leader, admitted that claims-made is the only way to go in this line of business.[43]

Given two years' retrospection, Rawls said that the medical malpractice insurance crisis taught regulators several lessons. Companies in the field did not have expertise. A very few cases caused the huge dollar loss. There was a lack of expertise handling claims. The insurance personnel might be handling "fender benders" one minute and medical malpractice the next. The rates were probably too low, and crises came from the suddenness of million-dollar verdicts and the decline of the stock market, events over which regulators had no control.[44]

It is obvious that under the present system the major carriers are not interested in underwriting medical malpractice coverage, which in their minds is an unprofitable and uninsurable risk. New ways to insure the risk must be found or steps must be taken to eliminate or restrict medical malpractice claims.

·◦] 2 [◦·

The Doctors' Lament

To MEMBERS OF THE MEDICAL PROFESSION, the malpractice issue goes far beyond consideration of the availability of insurance and the cost of malpractice premiums. Doctors feel that the quality of care they can render and their professional freedom to treat patients in a manner they deem best have been severely restricted as a result of the malpractice problem.

Malpractice is a very sensitive and emotional issue for doctors. Their outlook was succinctly summarized by Dr. Edward D. Henderson, chairman of the Professional Service Committee of the American Academy of Orthopedic Surgeons. Dr. Henderson said:

> Physicians are not, by and large, insensitive or callous. They are trained carefully to make decisions which are hard and are trained not to show their emotions. It has not been recognized generally that being sued by a patient . . . is a devastating occurrence. All of us have seen what it does to our colleagues. Even when they win the trial, they are no longer the incisive, effective optimistic surgeons which they were before. A court of law may be the workroom for the attorney, but it is the torture chamber for the doctor.[1]

A. Reynolds Crane, M.D., president of the Pennsylvania Medical Society, said: "Suing the doctor and the hospital is a new social disease. The cures for this disease must be broadly and equitably spread across society. Everyone sympathizes with the patient incapacitated by disease or injury, but this emerging de facto patient compensation program, improperly financed under the guise of the malpractice insurance system as we now know it, is destroying the ability of the physician and the hospital to take care of the sick."[2]

The complexities of modern medicine, doctors maintain, make it very difficult for a lay jury to judge the merits of medical

21

malpractice cases. One physician said: "Juries have the difficulty of determining the fact after listening to two opposing experts. The members of the jury don't know who is telling the truth but they can see a crippled man in a chair."[3]

Physicians' feelings on the malpractice issue have produced tremendous animosity toward lawyers. The conflict between doctors and lawyers was the subject of frank remarks by Chancellor Allen Wallis of the University of Rochester to the May 1974 graduates of the University's medical school:

> You who are receiving degrees in medicine . . . undoubtedly realize that throughout the country at this season thousands of others are receiving similar degrees in token of their preparation, like yours, for devoting the best parts of their lives to improving the health of their fellow men.
>
> Most of you are vaguely aware, also, that all over the country even larger numbers are emerging from professional schools of another sort, namely schools of law. Probably few of you realize, however, that before your careers have run their courses those lawyers may have more influence than you have over what you do, how you do it, and how you are rewarded.
>
> You may find lawyers defining the range of treatments that you are allowed to use in specified circumstances. Lawyers may prescribe the criteria by which you choose among the allowable treatments. Lawyers may specify the priorities you must assign to different patients. Lawyers may require you to keep detailed records to establish at all times that you are in full compliance. Lawyers may punish you unless you can refute . . . their presumption that your failures result from not following all of their rules, regulations, and requirements. And lawyers may decide what incomes you deserve.[4]

Some try to relate the increase in law school graduates from 9,240 in 1960 to 21,760 to the increase in medical malpractice claims.[5] Although the legal profession is considered to be a lucrative one by others, Ralph S. Emerson, M.D., president of the New York State Medical Society during the crisis year of 1975, said that lawyers today have economic fears. They are fearful of medical malpractice cases leaving the courtroom and ending up in arbitration. They are fearful that with no-fault automobile insurance here and no-fault for product liability on the horizon and medical no-fault now being discussed that their profession is being threatened.[6]

R. Crawford Morris, of Cleveland, a prominent malpractice defense attorney, endorses the often-heard contention by doctors that some lawyers are pursuing malpractice cases now to fill the vacuum created by no-fault. Morris, speaking at a State of Ohio Insurance Department hearing, said: "One lady in a hospital had a bug run across her face. She was all right, and her care was good; but four lawyers came in there and wanted her to file a suit."[7]

Morris' statement seemingly backs up another point—"medical information is leaking from hospitals to lawyers." John F. Dodge, Jr., a Michigan attorney, said: "One major hospital got rid of a snooping resident who was giving discharge data to lawyers, who would then contact the patients. We know there are people at hospitals who make a point of looking at discharge summaries, especially of patients undergoing complex procedures such as neurosurgery."[8]

Doctors are concerned about the long-range outlook for their own profession. The Federal Trade Commission and Congress have indicated that in the near future they are going to give close scrutiny to antitrust practices in medicine. The Senate Anti-Trust Committee planned to schedule hearings on this topic.[9] Chairman Michael Pertschuk of the Federal Trade Commission said: "There is reasonable doubt that the medical profession, by itself or through friendly state governments, is completely open to innovation, competition, quality control, or consumer choice."[10]

While doctors have been held in high esteem for centuries, from Shakespeare's time people have had negative feelings about lawyers. The work of an attorney is founded in controversy. A widely respected attorney in New York State recalled looking through some papers of a town in his area which dated back more than a hundred years ago. There was a notation that "it was a good year. We have neither a gypsy nor a lawyer in our town."[11]

The inability of state legislatures to resolve the malpractice problem quickly to their satisfaction has been a source of much irritation to many doctors. A physician who has observed legislative activities for several years said, "one of the problems of doctors in viewing the malpractice issue and the legislative process is their authoritarian attitude. In the hospital or in the office, the doctor issues an order to the nurse and others and they jump. The legislature doesn't."[12]

George Himler, M.D., a past president of the New York State Medical Society, pointed out that it is often the best doctors and those who take on the riskiest cases who are the targets of medical malpractice claims. Himler said: "Physicians who are innovative in their medical or surgical treatments and who have an unavoidably poor result are often penalized in malpractice litigation because their methods differ from the average care or norm in their areas. The rising incidence of malpractice suits, and concern over the resulting uprating of premiums, can effectively stifle the investigative attitudes on which progress in clinical medicine is based."[13]

A Rand Corporation research project prepared for the California Post-Secondary Education Commission confirmed that doctors in that state were altering their methods of practice. "An estimated 7 percent of insured physicians have made procedural changes—such as reducing, switching, or eliminating types of practice—to reduce their insurance premiums."[14] As many as 25 percent of insured family practice physicians have reduced the amount of surgery or obstetrics they perform. Obstetricians and gynecologists have cut back on their work in obstetrics, ear-nose-and throat specialists have decreased plastic surgery, radiologists were deciding to cut angiography and switch from therapeutic to diagnostic radiology.[15]

Medical research, doctors claim, is being limited by the threat of malpractice suits. Dwight Harken, M.D., of Boston, a pioneer in the use of the pacemaker in treating heart diseases, said, "the popular growing wave of consumerism plus the epidemic of malpractice suits" is deterring further advances in heart research.[16]

Duncan Barr, a San Francisco attorney who specializes in malpractice work, said that 280,000 people in this country have had heart valve surgery. Barr noted that 5,000 to 6,000 persons have died on the operating table or subsequently but that leaves another 275,000 people who have had heart valve surgery who are alive and who would not be were it not for the valve.[17]

Advances in medical research, ironically, are contributing to the increased number of malpractice suits. Tradition and accepted practices are being challenged in efforts to improve medicine. Years later, a doctor who followed a formerly accepted treatment or procedure, is sued because in retrospect the steps taken are no longer regarded as correct.

In some instances, juries tend to turn back the clock and forget to consider the state of medical knowledge at the time of the event in question. In other cases, newly discovered procedures may lead to results which were not predictable. Abortions and birth control pills are examples of the latter. Prior to recent years, most doctors did not have a great deal of experience on abortions. When birth control pills first were manufactured, no one said or foresaw what problems their use might produce.[18]

Pediatricians and others point to the use of heavy doses of oxygen for premature babies which was standard procedure twenty to thirty years ago. Now oxygen is recognized as contributing to RLF (retrolental fibroplasia), which produces blindness.

A classic example is that of Gail Kalmowitz who, at birth in 1953 at Brooklyn's Brookdale Hospital Medical Center, weighed only two and a half pounds. Twenty years later the blind young woman filed a malpractice suit alleging that the use of oxygen after birth resulted in blindness. In 1975, she accepted an out-of-court settlement for $165,000 which came while the jury was deliberating her case. It was subsequently revealed that the jury was ready to award her $900,000. The research study that confirmed a link between use of oxygen for premature babies and RLF was begun three months after Miss Kalmowitz was born in 1953. The study was not completed until 1966.[19]

The threat of malpractice claims and suits is blamed for the proliferation of what is called "defensive medicine," the ordering of additional laboratory tests, X-rays, drugs, and other precautions. Although some maintain that defensive medicine is good medicine, others argue that it is unnecessary and contributes significantly to the ever-escalating costs of health care.

Roger O. Egeberg, M.D., assistant secretary of health in the U.S. Department of Health, Education and Welfare, estimated in 1975 that the cost of defensive medicine was about $4 billion a year. Dr. Egeberg said, "There are people who have been studying it for about two or three years, and they have come up with criteria by which they judge it: the number of negative skull films, or the number of X-rays taken which were inferior substitutes for doctors' own judgment."[20] Seventy percent of physicians surveyed by the American Medical Association admitted they were ordering additional tests because of their concern about medical malpractice. Sixty-three percent of surgeons queried by the American College of Surgeons answered that they were "ordering X-rays for defensive purposes."[21]

Martin A. Gruber, M.D., president of the New York State Society of Orthopedic Surgeons, testifying at a legislative hearing, gave the following example of defensive medicine. Dr. Gruber said:

> Let us picture a man who has sustained a severe fracture of his ankle, perhaps while skiing on ice or even walking in the street. He is admitted to a hospital and a decision is made to operate and to fix his fracture with two stainless steel bone screws. We will assume

that his postoperative course is smooth, that he has been hospitalized about one week, and has been sent home in a cast with the screws still present in his ankle. About 10 to 12 weeks later these screws must be removed as they would otherwise interfere with the normal motion of his ankle. Fifteen years ago or so the usual procedure would have been to inject a local anesthetic about the patient's ankle and, in the physician's office, make two small simple incisions, remove the screws, and send the patient home. Total fee would be about $50. This is unthinkable today. The necessary criteria for legal defense of a case cannot be met in a physician's office and the patient must be hospitalized. The screws, therefore, will be removed in the operating room with an anesthesiologist standing by. The patient will be discharged from the hospital on the following day or perhaps two or three days later. Costs: surgeon's fee, $150 to $250; hospital fees, about $150 a day, let's say $350 for two days; operating room, an additional $50 to $150; anesthesiologist's fees, another $50, perhaps $100. Total cost: $500 to $750, 10 to 15 times what it would have otherwise been had our malpractice climate been different.

Who pays this cost? The public, of course.[22]

Critics of the medical profession maintain that unnecessary surgery has contributed to cases of medical malpractice. These charges have brought heated denials from doctors. James H. Sammons, M.D., executive vice-president of the American Medical Association, questioned the validity of second surgical opinions that are cited as proof that the surgery was unnecessary.[23]

Dr. Sammons said: "It is true it may save the insurance company or the government some money to deny a patient an operation through a 'second opinion' . . . but at what cost to the patient in terms of pain or discomfort? And who should make that decision— the patient, the patient's physician, a consultant, an insurance company, the government?"[24]

Hysterectomies have been labeled as procedures which are often unnecessary. Sammons pointed out to a congressional subcommittee that hysterectomy is used as a means of sterilization by some women and in some other cases as a means to limit the spread of cancer. Sammons commented: "I cannot believe that a Subcommittee of the Congress of the United States is going to tell the women of this country that they cannot or should not have an operation that could avoid the agony and ultimate death by cancer because, according to some abstract formula, it is not 'cost effective' and therefore unnecessary."[25]

Doctors are also quick to answer assertions that the increase in malpractice claims has led some to the conclusion that the quality of care is declining as indicated by this country's high infant and maternal death rate. Doctors counter that death figures are inaccurate because reporting in the United States is mandatory while in other countries it is not. America, they note, is the mecca of the world for the training of medical personnel and for outstanding medical facilities.

Disciplining of doctors, another subject raised by critics of the medical profession, is a sore point with physicians too. The doctors argue that "the medical profession has had the responsibility but no authority for disciplining its members." This topic will be covered in depth in chapter 5.

Doctors do not attempt to conceal the fact that malpractice does occur, but they seek to minimize the number of events. Robert W. Jamplis, M.D., president of the American Group Practice Association, said there are 300,000 physicians in the United States who see an average of 138 patients a week, producing two billion doctor-patient encounters a year. Dr. Jamplis added that 20,000 medical malpractice claims are filed, which averages out to one claim per 100,000 doctor-patient encounters.[26]

Dr. Jamplis listed three major reasons for the malpractice crisis:

1. Doctors are at fault for a breakdown in the doctor-patient relationship. He said there has been a breakdown in communications, a subject he feels should be taught in medical schools.

2. The Marcus Welby syndrome has produced a feeling in people that miracles can be performed in 60 minutes with time out for commercials.

3. Stories of large awards have spurred claims.[27]

Jamplis commented: "Any drug, any modality of treatment has dangers; and there will always be human errors in judgment, and undesirable results will continue to exist.[28]

Malcolm Todd, M.D., president of the American Medical Association in 1975, said all bad results which prompt legal suits are not, in his opinion, cases of malpractice. According to Dr. Todd, medical accidents do happen, and he recommended that a new system be developed which would respond to modern medicine of brain surgery, open heart surgery, and kidney transplants. He wants a system that is fair to the patients, the doctors, and the hospitals.[29]

Dr. Todd said: "The malpractice situation in many areas of this country has already had a serious detrimental effect on the doctor-patient relationship. It is very difficult for some physicians not to look upon a new patient as a potential litigant. Never mind that very few patients sue and very few doctors ever get sued. An adversary air has crept into the relationship and nobody is any better off for it. It actually impedes the practice of medicine."[30]

Surgery is more complex, Todd said, and there are some doctors practicing surgery who should not be, but, on the other hand, more cardiovascular patients are being returned to useful lives. He stated that people forget that anything done to a body involves risk. He said: "No doctor can guarantee success."[31]

The medical malpractice problem, as Assemblyman Barry Keene of California emphasized, is not a regional one. He said: "The crisis hit California, New York, Michigan, Indiana, and Florida at approximately the same time. It is not an urban-industrial problem alone . . . although those areas may be more susceptible because they have more specialists who are more separated from direct patient care, who are more exposed to high-risk patients, and who utilize more high-risk procedures."[32] Table 8 lists by specialty the ratio of claims pending in 1975 for all doctors in the country covered by St. Paul Fire and Marine Insurance company.

The squeeze in the availability of insurance can come anywhere and at any time, as physicians in New Mexico learned in 1975. Doctors insured by Travelers Insurance Company, carrier for the New Mexico State Medical Society, began that year on a pleasant note when Travelers reduced premiums by 15 percent. By summer Travelers received a 74 percent premium increase and then announced that its coverage for members of the Medical Society would be terminated on March 1, 1976.

Travelers had also decided to withdraw its coverage from Arizona doctors. Where the company did continue to insure doctors, its policyholders were hit with tremendous increases (486 percent in Southern California, 341 percent in Northern California and 271 percent in Texas).

Doctors' suspicions about insurance companies, coupled with the increasing difficulty of obtaining malpractice coverage, led them to set up their own insurance companies in some states. A few doctors have threatened to practice without insurance coverage, which is a risk to themselves, to their families, and to their patients. Nevertheless, some reportedly are doing so.

The payment of insurance premiums is one of many overhead expenses taken into account when a doctor establishes a fee

Table 8

SUMMARY OF MALPRACTICE CLAIMS PENDING
AGAINST INSUREDS OF THE ST. PAUL

Specialty	Ratio of Pending Claims
RATE CLASSIFICATION #1	
Allergist	1 per 26 doctors
Dermatologist	1 per 24
Hematologist	1 per 29
Internist	1 per 30
Pathologist	1 per 53
Pediatrician	1 per 37
Psychiatrist	1 per 44
Radiologist	1 per 14
Average: 1 per 29	
RATE CLASSIFICATION #2	
General Practitioner (Minor Surgery or assists in major surgery on own patients)	1 per 17
RATE CLASSIFICATION #3	
GP (Major Surgery)	1 per 12
Ophthalmologist	1 per 21
Proctologist	1 per 10
Average: 1 per 13	
RATE CLASSIFICATION #4	
Cardiac Surgeon	1 per 4
General Surgeon	1 per 7
Otolaryngologist (no plastic surgery)	1 per 9
Thoracic Surgeon	1 per 8
Urologist	1 per 11
Vascular Surgeon	1 per 5
Average: 1 per 7	
RATE CLASSIFICATION #5	
Anesthesiologist	1 per 8
Neurosurgeon	1 per 5
OB–GYN	1 per 6
Orthopedic Surgeon	1 per 5
Plastic Surgeon	1 per 6
Average: 1 per 6	

Source: "Preserving a Medical Malpractice Insurance Marketplace, Problems and Remedies," Position Paper and Backgrounder, St. Paul Fire and Marine Insurance Company, St. Paul, Minnesota, 1975, pp. 11–12.

schedule for his services. Actuaries forecast yearly premium increases of 20 to 30 percent unless drastic changes are made.

Specialists in high-risk categories—such as neurosurgery, orthopedics, and anesthesiology—are hardest hit by increases in malpractice premiums. In New York State, neurosurgeons and orthopedists paid an average premium of $659 in 1964 for a policy with limits of $100,000 and $300,000. By 1969 they were paying $2,225. In 1975, the same malpractice coverage cost $11,045.[33]

Many high-risk specialists raised the limits of their coverage to $1 million and $3 million because of increased lawsuits and higher awards. Such a policy cost $14,329 in the New York City metropolitan area during 1975.[34]

Although these specialists generally have incomes far exceeding those of other physicians, some doctors seek to make the case that it is unfair for the specialists to bear a heavier burden of malpractice costs. That case is made in the following testimony by an anesthesiologist.

> A question that arises is, "Should a specialist have greater liability than other physicians who take care of patients?" I do not believe that he should. The decision, for example, to do surgery is not the surgeon's alone. The patient is referred to him for surgery by a general practitioner or internist. There may be certain specialties which have greater built-in risks by virtue of what is being attempted for a patient. These are risks, not malpractice. In addition, such physicians work frequently in a hospital situation and their records and acts are available and exposed to all other individuals in the hospital with whom they work. They are now subject to peer review and utilization controls. The physician who practices in his office without supervision or control of any peer group may be guilty of long periods of gross malpractice simply because his acts are not exposed and the patient is not in a position to judge whether malpractice has occurred.[35]

William H. Bloom, M.D., a neurosurgeon in the suburban New York City area, said his malpractice premium of $15,000 represents 18 percent of his gross income. Dr. Bloom added that some of his colleagues "are paying in the vicinity of $30,000." He testified that in thirteen years of practice his malpractice premiums have increased 4,000 percent. At that rate, he projected, by 1986 his premiums would be about $250,000.[36]

Doctors practicing in states adjacent to Canada are quick to note the disparity in premiums between the United States and Canada. A general surgeon in Buffalo, New York, paid about $5,000 for his 1975 malpractice insurance while a general surgeon across the border in Toronto "doing the same work pays about $500."[37]

Doctors claim that states with high malpractice premiums are losing sorely needed medical personnel. Young physicians are choosing to locate in other states, while older practitioners are considering early retirement.

The Committee of Interns and Residents in New York State conducted a survey, "Will the current malpractice crisis force house staff officers to practice medicine outside of the State of New York?" Of more than 900 responses, "32 percent are now planning to leave New York State because of the current malpractice crisis. An additional 40 percent will probably be forced out for the same reason. Even before the current crisis arose, of those who did not consider practicing medicine in New York State, one-half had eliminated New York State because of existing exorbitant malpractice rates. Only 10 percent will be able to stay in New York State if the malpractice rates are increased."[38]

Ralph S. Emerson, M.D., president of the New York State Medical Society, said applications for the Brooklyn chapter of the American College of Surgeons were down almost 50 percent in 1975. For the past eight years the number of applicants had not varied more than 5 percent. Younger surgeons, he added, are leaving the state. Membership in the New York State Medical Society, however, has remained stable—which might indicate that the exodus of those already in practice does not involve large numbers of doctors.[39]

Several rural communities which have been experiencing great difficulty in attracting doctors to their area can be adversely affected by the malpractice issue. *Medical Economics* reported: "In Hasting, south of Grand Rapids (Michigan), a 10-year quest to attract family physicians seemed to have ended with the agreement of four medical school graduates to locate in the town. Unable to obtain malpractice insurance, the fleeing M.D.'s set up elsewhere."[40]

A 1977 report by the Rand Corporation indicates, however, that "the supply of California physicians had continued to rise despite some evidence of minor increases in the number moving out of the state to practice. . . . California medicine could be seriously affected if the medical malpractice controversy were to discourage medical graduate students in other states from coming to California to practice because the state depends heavily on physicians educated elsewhere."[41]

The report noted that 70 percent of practicing physicians in

California, excluding those employed by the federal government, were graduates of out-of-state medical schools.[42]

The malpractice issue has served to divide the ranks of the medical profession. A number of practitioners who believe that national, state, and county medical societies do not protect their best interests are challenging the leadership of these organizations and in several cases have established splinter groups.

One such group is the Michigan Physicians Crisis Committee whose "Court Docket Survey" summarizes the prevailing feelings of most doctors. Even the members of the medical establishment, whom this and other crisis committees are threatening, quoted from the survey when called upon to document their statements on the malpractice issue (see Appendix C for their conclusions). In its "Court Docket Survey" the group said:

> The Physicians Crisis Committee was born of frustration and disgust because in Michigan, and also nationally, the Hospital Associations and Medical Societies were in general disarray. Fearing regulation of their own, they hesitated to seek controls over others—and except when prodded by an ad-hoc group like the Physicians Crisis Committee—they continued a 20-year-old routine of arguing over how best to pass the rising insurance costs on to the public and working to achieve safe agreements with bar associations in an effort to preserve the status quo (don't ask to regulate me—I won't ask to regulate you).[43]

The Michigan survey was the end product of an examination of 2,754 cases filed. Michigan doctors and their counterparts in other states questioned the contingency fee arrangement between attorney and clients, whereby the attorney agrees to handle the case on the understanding that he or she will receive a predetermined amount of any award or settlement. If there is no award or settlement, the attorney receives no fee.

According to the Michigan Crisis Committee, the legal system in Michigan receives more than 50 cents of the malpractice premium dollar, while the patients get less than 25 cents. "Lawyers in Michigan, both plaintiffs' and defendants' counsel, were, in 1973–74, taking from the legal-jury system twice as much money as the injured patient."[44]

Norman S. Blackman, M.D., of Brooklyn, New York, a leader in New York State's crisis committee movement, said: "The contingent fee has made us the most litigious nation in the civilized world with antisocial results."[45]

David S. Rubsamen, M.D., a physician and attorney and a member of the HEW Medical Malpractice Commission, said that because of the increasing number of higher awards, the attorney "gets a chunk that is totally irrational."[46] In answer to those who say a lawyer invests a lot of time on malpractice cases, he said competent firms make an early judgment on the merits of a plaintiff's case. In 80 to 85 percent of the cases that are pressed, awards or settlements more than cover the time invested by the attorney.[47]

Dr. Rubsamen said:

> The contingent fee arrangement is a very sore point. When I speak to lawyers' groups, especially, I mention a prominent California law office which settled two cases, before trial, last fall, back to back, within six weeks of one another. In each of these cases, the negligence was quite obvious. The indemnity was $1,200,000 for one and $1,800,000 for the other. That law firm collected between the two cases something over $850,000 as a contingent fee. Does this not describe an irrationality in the system? A preservation of the contingent fee, I think, is rational, but adjusting it so that it will not bring such huge windfalls is also rational.[48]

The contingency fee is one of many legal issues of concern to doctors with respect to malpractice. Another, "informed consent"— what a patient must be told before undergoing a medical procedure or treatment—is of great concern to doctors.

The doctors' view of this issue is illustrated in the following testimony.

> Let's assume that somebody is seriously hurt and winds up in a hospital emergency room and this poor guy is scared to death. Everything is happening. There have been ambulances, people rushing around, he is in pain, he doesn't know what is happening, a doctor comes along. The purpose of the physician at this time, in addition to healing, ought to be to comfort. I should be able to step next to this person, and say, "Look, everything is going to be all right, don't worry, take it easy, you'll be fine." I can't say that. If I tell him everything is going to be all right, in another context, in a courtroom some day, that is guaranteeing a result. I have to essentially read him his rights like a policeman making an arrest. I have to tell him what the risks and potential benefits are of each surgical procedure that I plan to do. I have to explain to him what might occur. I have to list possibly even obtuse possible complications.
>
> Now, it is my obligation as a physician to choose what I think is best for my patient. I have to know all the risks and benefits of the procedure and, if I am going to be an ethical practitioner, I have no

right to propose anything except that. Nevertheless, there are certain occasions where this shouldn't be told to the patient, or at least not at the specific time and place because my primary responsibility has to be to the patient. As a doctor I am not supposed to be only a scientist and healer, I am supposed to be a comforter.

A physician frequently finds himself in the position of a surrogate parent, and the surrogate parent who wipes the tears away and says everything is going to be all right, shouldn't have to worry about a lawsuit at that time. This is placing a tremendous emotional burden on the physician and it get neglected in the physician-patient relationship which is suffering.[49]

Another practitioner, commenting on "informed consent," said, "It is a miracle people get doctors' instructions right. You can talk to patients but they may not listen and understand since they are often emotionally upset about their health when they see a physician."[50]

Other legal targets for doctors are the "ad damnum" clause and the doctrine of "res ipsa loquitur." The "ad damnum" clause requires a claimant to list a dollar amount he or she is seeking. Such a figure is in most instances much higher than the plaintiff expects to receive. Physicians argue that these figures in themselves establish an artificially high ceiling on awards for juries.

"Res ipsa loquitur" is a judicially established principle literally meaning "the thing speaks for itself." A prominent hospital administrator said:

> It has been generally applied in malpractice cases in selected circumstances; for example, the leaving of foreign objects in the patient's body after surgery, burns or other injuries suffered while the patient was under anesthesia, and so forth. The problem arises where res ipsa is permitted on a conditional basis if the jury accepts the circumstantial evidence underlying substandard medical conduct in rare accident cases. In these cases the question of negligence will be put to the jury without any expert medical testimony showing that the accused physician did actually depart from the accepted standard of care. A trend can be seen where res ipsa is being judicially expanded toward a point where the liability of health care providers is based solely on circumstantial evidence of negligence.[51]

The statute of limitations, the period of time in which to file a malpractice claim, varies from state to state. Prior to 1975, in many states malpractice claims involving actions taken against an infant could be filed up to twenty-one years or more after the event. Doctors think this lengthy period is unnecessary. One said: "I cannot think of any defect that would not turn up within a period of seven years after birth. . . . In five years a borderline brain damage might be missed. But by seven years, I think that anything would reasonably show up."

Many doctors have asked state legislatures to define medical malpractice by statute. The argument for a definition is as follows:

> The progressive enlargement and changing of theories of malpractice that have been produced by judge-made law, by court decisions, have made it impossible to determine in advance what an actionable tort in malpractice really is. Remember, there is a five-year delay. This makes defense more difficult and it encourages the development of defensive medicine. We doctors aren't lawyers, and so when we hear you have to have adequate records we assume if a little is good, more is better, and because we are in this emotional situation we overload on the keeping of records and the development of various kinds of medical tests that might conceivably be helpful. The patient and the public is paying for this and this is wrong, but it can't be righted until we know what we really do have to have.
>
> It is unfair to present a situation where somebody can be called to account for an act that he didn't really know was wrong. The legislature must make an adequate definition of what malpractice is.[52]

Doctors also favor placing a ceiling on awards, as has been enacted in a number of states.

Unrest within the medical profession about the malpractice issue seemed to aid efforts to unionize doctors. The American Federation of Physicians and Dentists, founded in January 1973, saw its membership double from 13,500 in October 1974 to 27,000 members in October 1975.

In 1975 the Physicians National House Staff Association, consisting of 18,000 of the nation's 60,000 interns and residents, voted to turn that group into a labor union. Among the demands of interns and residents is the right to strike.

The association president, Robert G. Harmon, M.D., said: "While many Americans have gained their impressions of hospital care by swallowing sugary placebos of Marcus Welby, the reality is that young house staff doctors have found that collective bargaining, and in some cases strikes, have been the only way they could force hospitals to provide such basic items as electrocardiogram machines that work, usable emergency equipment . . . and enough nurses to cover intensive care wards."[53]

Two chapters of the association went on strike during 1975. Interns and residents in Los Angeles County took part in a walkout at three hospitals in May. After the strike was settled they were granted wage increases and a fund was established to improve patient care. Interns and residents at twenty-three New York City hospitals struck in March and subsequently received a reduction in their work week from 110 hours to 80 hours.[54]

The American Medical Association, which has had a traditional anti-strike posture, issued a statement in support of the New York City interns and residents. Malcolm C. Todd, M.D., president of the AMA in 1975, said: "The malpractice problem is so critical that if the legislatures do not respond to remedial legislation we are absolutely going to have utter chaos in this country because for the first time in history you are going to see massive walkouts and withholding of services by American doctors."[55]

Strikes and work slowdowns were used in several states in an attempt to gain legislative approval of the doctors' solutions to the issue. While state legislatures later adopted some of the medical profession's proposals, physicians felt the legislative response was too little and too late.

·❧[3]❧·

What the Issue Means to Hospitals

THE 1974 REPORT of the California Assembly Select Committee on Medical Malpractice pointed out that "hospitals occupy a unique position in the malpractice controversy." The committee, headed by Henry A. Waxman, said hospitals "share with physicians the same concern about the tremendous rise in claims and verdicts. In fact, claims against hospitals are rising at a greater rate than claims against physicians. In the majority of malpractice suits brought today, the hospital is a codefendant."[1] The hospital is liable for the actions not only of the physicians but for all personnel, including nurses and technicians.

The HEW Commission on Medical Malpractice reported that "74 percent of all alleged malpractice incidents occur in hospitals."[2] Some say the figure is now closer to 85 percent.

Adrienne Astolfi, director of the hospital and health care sector of the National Commission on Productivity, said the effects of the malpractice issue on hospitals can be summarized in three points:

1. Hospitals are being severely criticized for their escalating costs, and yet the increases in their medical malpractice insurance are forcing those costs up further.

2. The present approach reduces quality of care.

3. The practice of defensive medicine on the part of their physicians forces hospitals to hire more people, purchase more equipment and material and thereby increases their costs.[3]

George B. Allen, president of the Hospital Association of New York State, claimed "that the public, the legislature and government agencies view malpractice primarily as a physicians' problem, with hospitals only remotely involved."[4]

37

Allen noted that in New York State "the amount of premiums paid by hospitals significantly exceeds that paid by physicians. It is our estimate that in 1974 hospitals paid about $75 million in premiums." He said many hospitals pay malpractice premiums for doctors on their staff. "If physicians find they are unable to practice without insurance coverage, . . . hospitals and patients suffer. Institutions must find ways to provide patient care, mainly on an emergency basis, and they must be able to absorb the financial adversities of empty beds since fixed costs continue."[5]

Table 9 lists the hospital malpractice premium experience for three representative hospitals in New York State. The same pattern of increased premiums is prevalent throughout most of the country.

Malpractice premiums for hospitals in this country, which ranged from $175 million to $200 million from 1967 to 1972, went from $250 million in 1973 to $350 million in 1974 to $750 million in 1975 and to $1.2 billion in 1976.[6]

The skyrocketing premiums made it virtually impossible for budget planners to project future malpractice costs. According to the American Hospital Association, original estimates made in 1973 of nationwide premium costs for hospitals for the year 1976 were $350 million. A year later the projections for 1976 were revised upward to $700 million. By 1975 the premiums for hospitals in 1976 were expected to be about $1 billion. As stated above, the 1976 premiums were actually $1.2 billion.[7]

Malcolm Todd, M.D., a past-president of the American Medical Association, cited the jump in malpractice premiums at Long Beach Memorial Hospital in his home community in California. Coverage which cost $14,000 in 1965 had risen to $820,000 in 1975.[8] Malpractice premiums for Denver General Hospital, which were $90,000 in 1975, went to $450,000 in 1976 and were expected to be $1 million in 1977. Colorado General Hospital, which paid $170,000 in 1975, saw its malpractice premiums soar to $377,000 in 1976 and was told to count on costs of $2 million in 1977.[9]

Michael Reese Hospital in Chicago had its malpractice insurance increased by 500 percent in one year. Senator Edward M. Kennedy said: "Those premiums are translated to a $10 average hike in the daily room costs" for patients at the hospital.[10]

In an attempt to reduce the ever-increasing cost of malpractice premiums some hospitals are resorting to self-insurance. St.

Table 9

HOSPITAL PREMIUMS
100-Bed Hospital

	1966	1970	1974
Malpractice premium	$16,000	$24,000	$278,000
No. of patient days	29,823	38,023	39,018
Cost of malpractice per day	0.536	0.631	7.12
Blue Cross/Blue Shield Reimbursement rate	44.76	71.36	104.88
Average length of stay	6.0 days	6.6 days	6.6 days

200-Bed Hospital

	1966	1970	1974
Malpractice premium	$ 7,000	$ 9,000	$119,000
No. of patient days	54,630	55,246	52,736
Cost of malpractice per day	0.128	0.163	2.26
Blue Cross/Blue Shield Reimbursement rate	Not Available	72.00 76.35	118.00 124.46
Average length of stay	7.5 days	6.1 days	5.9 days

600-Bed Hospital

	1966	1970	1974
Malpractice premium	$37,000	$50,000	$1,009,000
No. of patient days	157,399	191,126	191,629
Cost of malpractice per day	0.235	0.262	5.42
Blue Cross/Blue Shield Reimbursement rate	68.00	117.18	173.60
Average length of stay	12.5 days	11.5 days	11.1 days

Source: Data provided by the New York State Hospital Association, Albany, New York, to New York State Senate Health Committee, February 1975.

Luke's Hospital Center in New York City, for example, has self-insured the first $150,000 of its malpractice coverage since 1971.[11]

Hospital administrators considering self-insurance were not unmindful of the new perils that this route presented to them. Some of these concerns were expressed by Edward Messier, vice-president of St. Luke's:

> Those of us who are self-insured on malpractice now have a public liability problem. We have attempted to secure public liability

insurance that would have exclusionary language applicable to malpractice but have not met with much success. In deciding whether to go self-insured or not, we felt confident that, with our claim experience, this was the way to go. The day after we made that decision, we got a bomb scare and that made us begin to think twice about public liability. We have not been able to secure, at a reasonable rate, public liability insurance. We have every reason to believe that the very same liability carriers that are not giving us malpractice insurance are not willing to write public liability insurance and those of them that seem willing are perhaps "class b carriers." The rates connected to premiums and coverage are as equally exorbitant as they were under malpractice.[12]

James L. Groves, risk manager for the American Hospital Association, advised hospitals to make a comparison between self-insurance and commercial insurance.[13]

Hospital associations in several states set up their own insurance companies. The American Hospital Association pointed to the Hospital Association of Pennsylvania's company as its most successful operation with 120 member-hospitals.[14]

Off-shore companies are another technique being tried by hospitals in an attempt to obtain malpractice coverage at reduced rates. A group of twelve hospitals in the Boston area banded together to form the Harvard Medical Institutions Insurance Association which is officially called the Controlled Risk Insurance Company Ltd. (CRICO). In 1976 CRICO was chartered in the Cayman Islands in the British West Indies. This operation was set up off shore not only because of the absence of Massachusetts legislation permitting establishment of an in-state company but also to avoid federal income taxes on underwriting and investment profits. It is estimated that the firm saves approximately $2 million each year by taking advantage of the off-shore tax shelter.[15]

The company underwrites medical malpractice and general liability insurance for the twelve institutions and their affiliated physicians. Premiums for the policy year beginning April 1, 1977, were $6,050,111. Its investment portfolio was approximately $5 million.[16]

The American Hospital Association set up its own firm, the Health Providers Insurance Company as a backup. This company would become functional upon the request of at least ten state hospital associations having a total of 300 hospitals, 30,000 beds, and $10 million in premiums.[17]

As hospitals began to explore new ways to obtain malpractice coverage through self-insurance or companies established by state hospital associations, the federal government was very slow to change Medicare reimbursement to take into account these alternatives for hospital malpractice insurance. In fact, it was not until the winter of 1977 that the Medicare reimbursement formula was modified in a way to assist hospitals who sought new and in most instances less expensive means of obtaining continued malpractice coverage.

While malpractice poses problems for all hospitals, those affiliated with medical schools have experienced additional hardships. These were defined by J. Robert Buchanan, M.D., dean of the Cornell University Medical College and president of the Associated Medical Schools of New York. Dr. Buchanan said:

> A. the malpractice crisis encourages physicians to practice "defensive medicine," which runs counter to what we are trying to teach in our medical schools;
>
> B. people in part-time activity are withdrawing from practice;
>
> C. physician faculty in the medical schools which do not have their own hospitals are especially vulnerable since the only feasible way for them to get coverage is through a hospital;
>
> D. medical schools have unusual liability exposure since they are responsible for the actions of medical students and other trainees, perhaps even when in a clinical setting in another state. We should not be penalized for assuming this extra burden.[18]

In testimony before the New York State Governor's Special Advisory Panel on Medical Malpractice, Dr. Buchanan said:

> 1. A differential, effort-related premium is the only equitable method of insuring a physician who spends most of his time in teaching and administrative duties.
>
> 2. The escalation of malpractice insurance rates is causing physicians to leave our state. This is frustrating the public policy goal of increasing the aggregate number of doctors and the efforts of the medical schools to meet this perceived need by increasing their enrollments.
>
> 3. The new rates will put great strain on the teaching hospitals, without whom quality medical education is impossible.[19]

Hospital administrators maintain that malpractice litigation has adversely affected the operation of hospitals and has contributed to the rising number of claims and awards.

In its preliminary report in June 1974 the California Assembly Select Committee on Medical Malpractice said: "Years ago most hospital liability originated from what may be described as physical mishaps. Patients falling out of their beds was a common example. Very few claims arose from the actual practice of medicine. In other words, there was a time when hospital liability was significantly different than physician medical malpractice."[20]

A report prepared for HEW in 1975 pointed out that "in the past, doctrines of charitable immunity, the force of social custom and wide ignorance of medical error protected the hospital against suit." The report further stated:

> After enactment of Medicare and Medicaid, however, hospitals began garnering public funds for the care of some patients formerly treated free of charge. Often in fact and more often in the perception of the public, many hospitals then lost their charitable character. Accordingly, existing doctrines of charitable immunity were overridden in many areas of the country. Concurrently, newspapers, magazines, radio, and television publicized instances of medical error, raising public awareness of possible occasions for suing the hospital, the doctor, or both. The necessary condition for hospital liability had been established and the sufficient causes for suit, dramatized.
>
> At present, the hospital sector is described as struggling to comprehend and provide for the new magnitude of its liability. In any event, the scope of hospital liability will always remain uncertain, being subject to court decisions and legislative enactments and the trends established thereby. For instance, the landmark Nork decision made it plain that hospitals could expect to bear responsibility for the competence of their attendings as well as that of full-time employees. Given liability of such untold scope, it is difficult in the extreme to evaluate and reduce the severity of risk.[21]

The aforementioned California case, *Gonzales v. Nork*, "imposed a far-reaching doctrine of 'corporate responsibility' on a Sacramento hospital failing to discover the defendant physician's propensity to commit medical malpractice."[22]

In his decision, Superior Court Judge Abbott Goldberg said: "The hospital has a duty to protect its patients from malpractice by members of its medical staff when it knows or should have known that malpractice was likely to be committed upon them. The hospital had no actual knowledge of Dr. Nork's propensity to commit malpractice, but it was negligent in not knowing. It was negligent in not knowing because it did not have a system of acquiring knowledge."[23]

The California Assembly Select Committee commented: "Although this portion of the Nork decision has now been rendered moot by a settlement, if it is followed in subsequent cases, it could extend tremendously the liability of hospitals for medical malpractice."[24]

Another notable California case impacting on hospitals was a $4 million award against Mount Zion Hospital. "The doctor was found negligent for not examining the patient (Kelly Niles) before advising the on-duty intern and resident that the boy be discharged in the custody of his father. Although the pediatrician was not acting as a salaried hospital employee at the time of the Niles patient encounter, the hospital was still considered liable for not having adequate medical care monitoring mechanisms in operation."[25]

The practical implications of these court decisions for hospitals were outlined by Monsignor James Fitzpatrick, vice-president and director of government relations for the Hospital Association of New York State.

> This form of liability can be properly labeled as institutional liability for the competence of the medical staff, and applied equally to employees and non-employees, that is, those pursuing the private practice of medicine. This legal theory is based on the responsibility of hospitals to assure the public, to the best of their ability, that physicians practicing within the hospital are medically competent. Thus, if a hospital knows, has reason to know, or even should have known, of potential incompetence of a physician, then the hospital is liable to the patient for the negligence of the physician. Every time a hospital extends privileges to a physician, that institution assumes liability for his actions in that institution.
>
> Further, it has become common practice that complaints against a physician based on alleged medical malpractice within the hospital will include the hospital as a codefendant, even though the hospital's liability is unfounded. Although the hospital may be dismissed as a codefendant, a reserve will have already been set up by the insurance carrier that affects subsequent premiums.[26]

At the national and state level, hospital associations, individual hospitals and hospital trustees became active in attempts to seek legislative changes to alleviate the malpractice problems for hospitals, the medical profession and to better serve injured parties.

While legislators were suspicious of doctors, insurance companies and trial lawyers, and begrudgingly moved to adopt any measures to assist these groups, hospitals were seen as one segment of the problem that they really wanted to help.

The movement to assist hospitals was aided by the fact that in many instances hospitals have replaced doctors' offices as the focal point of the health care delivery system. In some states where physician slowdowns, work stoppages, or strikes have occurred, hospital service was dramatically affected. This situation posed a tremendous threat to the well-being of Americans, and is perhaps the most compelling reason for legislatures to continue efforts to seek more meaningful and effective solutions to the malpractice problem.

·◦[4]◦·

Doctors Blamed for the Crisis

I N ANSWER TO CHARGES by doctors and others that the legal profession
has created the malpractice crisis, the plaintiff's bar countered
that the negligent acts of physicians are the real cause of the crisis.

Richard M. Markus, a member of the HEW Medical Malpractice Commission and later appointed to the American Bar Association's Commission, said that doctors are "paranoid about the so-
called malpractice menace."[1] Markus quipped: "You doctors really
aren't being persecuted. Neither the law nor your patients are out to
get you. Malpractice actions are rare indeed, and rarer still are
those that defeat the physician. But if there's any reason at all to
fear them, my advice to you is: Don't look over your shoulder to see
who's after you. Take, instead a better look at yourself."[2]

Trial lawyers argue that they are merely defending the rights
of injured patients. Robert E. Cartwright, a California attorney who
was president of the Association of Trial Lawyers of America in
1975, said: "The patients' welfare and rights seem to be completely
ignored and don't seem to matter."[3] Cartwright contended that doctors want specialized dispensation although they, themselves, he
said, have been responsible for the malpractice crisis.

Richard E. Shandell, chairman of the Medical Malpractice
Committee of the New York State Trial Lawyers Association, Inc.,
claimed: "The physician has traditionally been the most unsuper-
vised and unregulated member of our society. But the age of consumerism has finally caught up with the physician. Accountants,
architects, home builders, auto manufacturers and others have all
learned in recent years that the old days when they did what they
pleased are gone. The physicians are slower to reconcile themselves
to this and like it no more than General Motors."[4]

Robert Begam, president of the Association of Trial Lawyers of America for 1976, blamed doctors and insurance companies for the malpractice crisis. Begam stated that the increase in malpractice premiums was a result of "maniacal greed" of the carriers, efforts by the insurance companies to recoup their stock market losses and the "frightening incompetence of too many health care providers." Doctors and the insurance industry, he said, have "tarred and feathered the trial lawyers and made the trial bar the scapegoat for their own misdeeds."[5]

In 1977, the District Attorney's office in Anchorage, Alaska, conducted an investigation into "allegations that physicians in Anchorage have conspired to refuse treatment to certain attorneys and their families." An assistant attorney-general in the State of Alaska's Department of Law said that some physicians deny the conspiracy while others do not. The charges center on claims that some doctors refused to treat families of lawyers who are handling malpractice cases against doctors.[6]

New Jersey Insurance Superintendent James J. Sheeran said: "What's bugging them [doctors] is the tort liability system, which tells them that they can be held responsible for the injuries that their incompetence can cause to a patient. They would rather change an old-time tested system of reparations in favor of reforms that would make of medical practitioners an even more privileged class than they already are."

Sheeran added:

> They want a limit on the size of a malpractice award. Knock somebody down with your auto, and the amount of money that a jury can assess against you is unlimited. But the doctors want a limit put on the results of their malpractice.
>
> They want to change the statute of limitations to further constrict the right of an injured patient to sue, even though the sponge left in the abdominal cavity by an absent-minded surgeon may not be discovered until years after the operation.
>
> They want the jury system replaced by an arbitration panel, dominated by the doctors themselves, of course. That is tantamount to letting the fox guard the chicken coop.
>
> In pursuance of these unworthy aims, medical professionals have sometimes rattled sabres in a manner that would do credit to the most militant of unions.[7]

A former state insurance commissioner of Pennsylvania, Herbert S. Denenberg, joined Sheeran in attacking doctors. Denenberg said: "Don't forget that the American Medical Association and state medical societies have waged a continuous battle to cover up malpractice and to shield members of their fraternity from criticism. There is also a conspiracy of silence among the medical profession when it comes to testifying against another practitioner. If anything, we should be lengthening the statute of limitations and making it easier to prove malpractice."[8]

Speaking on behalf of trial lawyers, Robert Cartwright said: "From the very beginnings of our country our moral and legal philosophy has been that people should be held accountable, yes, responsible for their wrongs and that immunity breeds irresponsibility. We have felt that if one person wrongs another that he should have to pay, regardless of whether he is a lawyer, doctor, engineer, accountant, or private citizen." Malpractice suits, he maintained, have been effective in improving health care. He pointed to sponge counts, instrument counts, electrical grounding of anesthesia machines, the padding of shoulder bars on operating tables, and the avoidance of colorless sterilizing solutions in spinal anesthesia agents as safety steps which have been inaugurated because of successful medical negligence cases. Cartwright outlined "a few specific case examples which illustrate the justice to the individual victim and the benefit to society of the tort system."[9] He cited six cases.

1. There is the case of the little girl who went in for a tonsillectomy operation. The anesthesiologist mishandled the anesthesia and the little girl blew up like a tire, with the result that her lungs ruptured and the little girl died.

2. There is the case of the woman patient who had the cancerous kidney. The attending surgeon read her X-rays backwards and took out her good kidney, leaving her only with a cancerous kidney and a very short life expectancy.

3. From my own state of California there is the case of the man who went into the hospital for an amputation of his leg at the same time that another man went in for an orchiectomy (removal of a testicle). The doctor removed the testicle from the man who was supposed to have his leg amputated.

4. There are the volksmann contracture cases—the so-called "too tight cast" cases—as a result of which gangrene would set in and the victims would lose their legs or their arms. We seldom see such suits any more because of the successful lawsuits which brought this problem to light.

5. There are the retrolental fibroplasia cases—the excessive oxygen given to premature babies, as the result of which blind-

ness occurred. Once again, we seldom see such cases any more because of the successful lawsuits which resulted.

6. The final example which I would like to cite is the recent celebrated case from Sacramento, California, involving the infamous Dr. Nork. This doctor, an alleged drug addict, for over ten years performed unnecessary back operations in an incompetent and bungled fashion, resulting in the butchery of over fifty persons. . . . It was a trial lawyer, Mr. Edward Friedberg from Sacramento, under the contingency fee system, who, through weeks and months of digging and investigating, unearthed what this monster was doing. Thereafter, he successfully achieved a large settlement against the hospital following a substantial award against Dr. Nork, both for compensatory and punitive damages, not from a jury, but from a trial judge.[10]

In testimony at a New York State Legislative hearing, Lee E. Goldsmith, a New York City attorney who also holds an M.D., said: "Generally speaking the lawsuits reflect the same medical problems or mistakes, if you will, occurring time and time again. All will agree clamps should not be left behind, but when they are, why is the error compounded and cost driven skyward? . . . Yet time and time again these patients have been required to pay a second surgical fee to have the offending foreign body, mistakenly left behind, removed. It's incredible."[11]

In discussing increased malpractice premiums for physicians, trial lawyers, consumer groups, and others say that the premiums for doctors are not exorbitant when one considers the physician's income. An orthopedic surgeon, it is noted, may make $200,000 a year. He may have to pay $20,000 for his malpractice premium but that amount is deductible from his taxes. Because of this deduction, the case could be made that the government is actually subsidizing about 50 percent of malpractice premiums.

The general practitioner, even in a high-risk state such as New York, was paying only about $1,200 to $2,400 a year in malpractice premiums in 1977.

It is also argued by some that Americans receive poor quality care. The number of neonatal and maternal deaths and the number of malpractice suits in this country, as opposed to those in Canada and England, are used as examples.

When asked to explain the increase in malpractice claims, Cartwright listed five reasons:

1. There has been a breakdown in the doctor-patient relationship because of increased specialization.

2. Many more people are obtaining medical care because of Medicaid and Medicare.

3. Our increasingly consumer-oriented society does not wish to tolerate inferior products or inferior health care.

4. The news media are responsible for increased consumer awareness.

5. Courts have become fed up with the conspiracy of silence by doctors which has made it difficult to obtain medical testimony.[12]

New York Attorney Herman Glaser has labeled today's impersonal doctor-patient relationship "turnstile medicine." He said: "You go into a doctor's office, four rooms, four patients, one doctor, and he is going from one room to the other. Mistakes are going to happen under those circumstances, and doctors are too busy today."[13]

Many people are resentful of doctors for many reasons. They claim doctors are aloof. They resent that doctors take a day off in the middle of the week when most other people are working. They hold it against doctors that their practices are lucrative. The age of medical specialties has made the doctor-patient relationship in many instances a very fleeting one. The surgeon may be a person the patient has met only once prior to surgery.

Failure to communicate adequately with patients, is a frequent complaint. Such was the case involving a general practitioner and a female patient. The patient was told that a routine X-ray taken during a physical examination revealed a large growth that was resting upon the spine. The doctor said he would refer the X-ray to a specialist. The patient returned to her home more than a hundred miles away with her husband, who had a heart condition. Five days went by and they heard no word from the doctor. Finally they called the physician who said "everything is all right," and offered no explanation for the false alarm which gave the patient, her husband, and two children hours and days of unnecessary worry.

An eye doctor who had been treating a patient for four years removed cataracts from both eyes in separate operations. Following the second operation he failed to give the patient a checkup of both eyes before he ordered contact lenses. When this mistake was discovered the patient had to return the contact lenses, which the company fortunately accepted without charge, and then had to wait two more weeks to get his new contact lenses. The doctor did not apologize or in any way acknowledge the inconvenience that he had caused the patient including a round trip of 250 miles from his home.

These may be isolated instances but they happen enough to cause some people to think that some doctors are either insensitive, unthinking or both. Just as public officials suffer from the acts of a few, these actions by doctors prompt many persons to generalize about the entire medical profession.

A shortage of physicians, attributed to the medical profession's efforts to preserve a closed fraternity (called "professional birth control") has contributed to the malpractice problem. Shandell explained this reasoning at a New York legislative hearing. He said:

> For generations organized medicine has acted to hold down the number of medical school graduates in the interest of creating an artificial scarcity of physicians so as to achieve great affluence for those remaining.
>
> The shortage is so acute that we are treated to the spectacle of whole areas bidding for the services of an immigrant Vietnamese physician plucked out of that war. We are treated to the startling sight of this gentleman grasping a copy of Harrison on Internal Medicine and promising to study how to pass his exams so that he could take the post. We saw none from General Motors recruiting any immigrants, elementary engineering text in hand, to design automobiles. But that is the best sort of doctor to which those poor folks in Nebraska could aspire.
>
> As a result of this conspiracy to hold down the number of medical graduates, bright American students are unable to gain admission to our American medical schools and either have to give up their dream of becoming a physician or go ahead to foreign medical schools to study. We are regularly importing large numbers of semi-educated foreign medical doctors who have graduated from primitive medical schools in undeveloped countries to serve as a primary source of medical care in most of our hospitals. . . .
>
> The doctor shortage also results in inadequate coverage during the off-hours. A large percentage of malpractice cases falls into the pattern of what I like to call Sunday cases. Sunday cases don't always happen on Sunday; they happen late at night or on Wednesday afternoons or any weekend or any holiday. Because, although the obligations of physicians are on a 24-hour-a-day seven-day-a-week basis, nobody works 24 hours a day, seven days a week, and there simply aren't enough physicians to go around, to cover around the clock.[14]

The great number of rejections by students seeking admittance to medical schools is another factor which some feel adds to a negative attitude toward the medical profession. Each year approximately 42,000 men and women apply to medical schools, and only 15,000 are admitted, leaving nearly 30,000 applicants, their families, and friends "who hate the AMA, in spite of the fact that the AMA has contributed $73 million in student guaranteed loans."[15]

Although medical experts claim there are enough doctors in the United States, many citizens in isolated rural areas or even heavily populated urban settings often have trouble finding a doctor when they need one. It is obvious that more physicians must be attracted to what may be less exciting practices in rural communities or, the other extreme, inner-city areas. In many localities, the private sector and government have joined forces to provide the necessary incentives for medical school graduates, but much work remains to be done.

Cartwright is among those who cite unnecessary surgery as a major cause in the increase of malpractice claims, claiming there are two million unnecessary surgery procedures per year.[16] Some contend that there are about 10,000 deaths each year which are the result of unnecessary operations.

Eugene G. McCarthy and Geraldine W. Widner reported in the New England Journal of Medicine the results of a study by the Cornell University Medical College Department of Public Health. The surgical experiences of 1,356 members of two labor unions were monitored for periods ranging from 23 to 28 months. Approximately 24 percent of the elective or non-emergency operations recommended to the union members were deemed unnecessary upon reexamination by board-certified specialists. Of those unnecessary procedures 40.3 percent were orthopedics, 38.5 percent urology; 31.4 percent gynecology, 28.2 percent ophthalmology; 16.4 percent general, and 16.3 percent ear, nose, and throat.[17]

McCarthy and William M. Stahl, M.D., professor of surgery at New York University Medical School, told a congressional committee that there are three million unnecessary operations each year which cost Americans between $3 and $4 billion. The two doctors said surgeons are "more concerned with making a good living than with helping their patients."[18]

The House of Representatives Oversight and Investigations Subcommittee released data showing that "poor and medically needy whose health bills are paid by Medicaid undergo twice as much surgery as the rest of the population." The findings were based on information obtained from twenty-six states.[19]

A team of four Harvard medical professors in another study

completed in 1977 contended that "many of the 20 million operations performed on Americans each year were of questionable surgical value, and that their cost was adding substantially to health care costs." The doctors cited a 14 percent increase in the number of operations performed since 1967.[20]

The results of a study released in the spring of 1977 claimed that one-third of the deaths resulting from operations were preventable, as were nearly one-half of the critical incidents among surgical patients. The study, conducted by Dr. Charles Child of the University Hospital, Ann Arbor, Michigan, was authorized by the American College of Surgeons. Hospitals in seven states (Connecticut, Maryland, Michigan, North Carolina, Ohio, Pennsylvania, and Washington) took part in the project.[21]

Representatives of consumer groups and trial lawyers who address themselves to the topic of defensive medicine state that "defensive medicine is good medicine" or seek to play down its influence on the total issue of medical malpractice. The latter group often refers to a research project, "The Malpractice Threat: A Study of Defensive Medicine," which involved selected physicians in California and North Carolina: "The threat of a malpractice suit does induce physicians to overutilize diagnostic tests and procedures in particular cases, but the survey results support the tentative conclusion that the practice is not extensive and probably not a contributing factor to the rising costs of medical care."[22]

Shandell said: "Extra tests are being ordered as a substitute for careful history taking and careful clinical examination. Doctors are getting into trouble in malpractice suits not because they didn't order a whole battery of tests but because they didn't take the pains and the care to listen to their patients."[23]

David S. Rubsamen, M.D., a California internist and a lawyer and editor of the *Professional Liability Newsletter,* said defensive medicine is costly but in the long run it results in savings in terms of monetary concerns and human suffering.

Charges by doctors about contingency fees are a "red herring" to Cartwright: "Since the beginning of our country the contingency fee has been the key to the courthouse for the ordinary citizen." The California attorney claimed that people are not complaining about contingency fees. He referred to figures compiled by the California Bar Association about all complaints filed against lawyers. According to Cartwright, only one complaint concerned itself with contingency fees. He said contingency fees act as a deterrent for lawyers to take on only meritorious cases.[24]

Appearing at a United States Senate hearing, J. Robert Hunter, Jr., acting Federal Insurance Administrator, Federal Insurance Administration, said: "New Jersey has had limitations for a long time on contingency fees, a sliding scale approach. Yet they still have a malpractice problem."[25]

In his statement to two New York State Legislative Committees, Lee S. Goldsmith, a doctor and an attorney, said: "For physicians to state that lawyers' fees should be regulated severely is tantamount to their agreeing all fees should be regulated. . . . It would be delightful (as a lawyer) to start a malpractice case knowing you would be repaid, at any scale, for your work. There would be ten times the present level of lawsuits against doctors. Today accepting a lawsuit against a doctor, even those that may look highly justified, is still somewhat of a gamble."[26]

The Court Docket Survey by the Michigan Physicians' Crisis Committee, described in Chapter 2, as expected drew a sharp response from the lawyers in that state. Michael Franck, executive director of the State Bar of Michigan, said the survey "is a classic case of how an organization born of what its principals see as a crisis tried after the 'crisis' has subsided to justify (1) its past rhetoric, and (2) its continued survival."[27]

Joining the bar in criticism of the Crisis Committee's Docket Survey was the Medical Protective Company. At a March 31, 1977, hearing on insurance rates for anesthesiologists, the company said: "The only value which we find in this local survey is the lesson to be learned from attempting to utilize irresponsibly small data bases which lack statistical credibility."[28]

Franck said that cooperation between the medical and legal professions over a six-month period helped greatly in efforts to pass legislation in that state to cope with the malpractice problem. "The current attempt to resurrect the atmosphere of confrontation which prevailed last summer and fall is so irresponsible as to border upon the incredible." Discussion of the contingency fee was no longer important since the State's Supreme Court upon the recommendation of the Michigan Bar Association had adopted rules reducing attorneys' fees. The Physicians' Crisis Committee's own figures, Franck pointed out, show that "in 90 percent of the cases, a recovery was obtained, thereby demonstrating how carefully and effectively lawyers and the contingency fee screen valid cases from those which lack merit." The Crisis Committee's attempt to link a rise in malpractice suits to the enactment of no-fault automobile insurance was criticized by Franck. In 1972, prior to no-fault, he said, "there was a substantial increase in malpractice cases." In California, where the malpractice crisis has been the most severe, "that state did not and does not have auto no-fault."[29]

A report to Michigan Governor William G. Milliken in 1975 also disavowed any connection between no-fault automobile insurance and the malpractice crisis: "A comparison of one company's experience in Michigan, Ohio, Pennsylvania, Texas, and Illinois indicated that the increase between 1973-74 in numbers of claims per insured by risk classification is virtually the same for all the states. Michigan is the only auto no-fault state of the five states used in the comparison."[30]

Trial lawyers like Shandell attempt to dispel the need for a definition of medical malpractice, which is strongly suggested by doctors: "Malpractice is clearly and precisely defined by the existing case law." Shandell added:

> What is more, the physicians have already built into the law a special immunity. The negligence of a physician may be established only by testimony that the physician's treatment fell below standards for such care and treatment generally accepted by his fellow physicians. . . . Demands for redefinition of the law with regard to the definition of malpractice are thus demands for immunity from responsibility for negligence, an immunity possessed by no other segment of our society including the sovereign.[31]

While doctors claim that juries are unable to make intelligent decisions on the complexities of malpractice cases, trial lawyers defend juries and the jury system. Shandell said: "Juries do understand malpractice cases and come to be able to grasp the significance of all of the items of medical evidence put before them in the course of a long and complex trial frequently better than some of the physician witnesses who come late into the trial. . . . The usual issue in a malpractice case then is not what proper medical care required but who is telling the truth about the underlying facts."[32]

Another legal question, the doctrine of informed consent, is one of great concern to consumer groups but their focus differs from that of physicians discussed in Chapter 2. The Committee on Patients' Rights, a New York-based organization, said: "Until the patient's right to know is recognized by law medical malpractice lawsuits will proliferate." The committee said:

> Informed consent, based upon what a reasonable patient would want to know, can eliminate one of the major causes of medical malpractice lawsuits—the anger or resentment of the injured or disappointed patient when the patient realizes that he or she has been subjected to or damaged by a treatment in which there were identifiable but undisclosed risks. The failure of the physician to offer to disclose to the patient, prior to treatment, the risks, hazards, length of disability, possibility of failure, and important areas of uncertainty regarding the delayed or long-term effects of the proposed treatment is a major cause of malpractice suits.[33]

The elimination of the doctrine of "res ipsa loquitur" is opposed by trial lawyers, although they admit that the doctrine is rarely applied in malpractice cases. Shandell said: "It does seem, however, wrong in principle to eliminate it since it applied only to the most outrageous and transparent sort of case. Occasionally it is essential. How else could one establish a case when one's 2-day old infant emerges from the nursery with a maimed limb?"[34]

The lack of effective patient grievance mechanisms has been a concern of many individuals and organizations. The Feminist Health Research Committee said: "We are of the opinion that the existing patient grievance mechanisms are not adequate because the majority of medical consumers are not all aware of their existence."[35]

Lee S. Goldsmith said: "It becomes quickly apparent to those who will see that there is a tremendous dissatisfaction with much of modern medical care when the result is untoward. Doctors do not seem to be able to explain negative results to patients. Unhappy people consult lawyers. They never teach you to handle the disgruntled patient in medical school."[36]

Although the news media for the most part have been supportive of the medical profession's attempts to seek changes in existing law regarding malpractice, doctors have lost their status of being immune from the criticism of editorial and headline writers. Strikes and the threatened withdrawal of services have aroused journalists and other segments of the general public.

An attorney who has been part of efforts to seek cooperation between the legal and medical professions on the issue of medical malpractice believes that doctors are losing status for a number of reasons including a preoccupation with business and investments.

The mercenary aspects of the practice of medicine were high-lighted in a headline, "M.D. Means Many Dollars," which accompanied an editorial in the *Syracuse* (New York) *Post-Standard*, July 11, 1975. The article was critical of the opposition of doctors and dentists to federal legislation which would force them to pay back some of the federal funds given to their schools to pay for their education. The editorial stated: "The would-be physicians threaten that any money they have to pay back to the federal government will ultimately have to be paid back by their future patients through increased fees. It is a nice threat from a group which has prided itself on a high standard of ethics and 'professionalism.'"

Among critics of doctors, perhaps the most often-heard complaint centers on doctors' unsuccessful attempts to discipline their colleagues. Herbert S. Denenberg said: "The self-policing of the medical profession has been a failure and a fraud and any malpractice solution should strengthen public control over a profession gone awry."[37]

Disciplining of Doctors—Does It Exist?

T HERE IS NO UNIFORM SYSTEM for the disciplining of doctors in the United States. This responsibility in a majority of states is vested in state boards of medical examiners, which are separate, self-governing agencies. In a few states the boards of medical examiners are under the supervision of departments of licensure; in other states the boards are within the departments of health or education.[1]

Regardless of where jurisdiction lies, disciplining of doctors has for the most part been ineffective—one of the few aspects of the malpractice issue on which insurance companies, doctors, attorneys, hospital administrators, and consumer advocates agree. These groups, however, do not agree on the reasons for this ineffectiveness.

Some doctors who have sought to take an active role in the disciplining process have encountered problems such as those mentioned by John J. Coury, M.D., a member of the American Medical Association's Council on Legislation. Dr. Coury said: "I sat on a licensing board for eight years with regard to physicians and their competence and every time we tried to take an action, we were frustrated by the legal profession, and the attorney-general's office. In some instances, when we did suspend a physician's license, he eventually gained it back through the courts."[2]

Edward Siegel, M.D., deputy executive vice-president of the New York State Medical Society, reported that "we are often accused of not cleaning our own house." Siegel added, "if we are to police our own, we want the same authority that lawyers have and we need immunity for those sitting on review boards."[3]

Supporting Siegel and others was a statement by the American Insurance Association that "medical societies are not authorized by law to discipline doctors." Although many states have enacted legislation which requires insurance carriers to provide information on malpractice claims, most of these new laws "provide that this information should be confidential and available only to the department of health and to the insurance department." The insurance industry organization referred to the establishment of Professional Standards Review Organizations (known as PSROs) as an important development in the disciplining of doctors. "These local physician groups are directed to review medical treatment cases where federal reimbursement is sought."[4] The federal legislation, which was part of the Social Security Amendments of 1973, gives doctors taking part in PSROs immunity which should encourage greater participation in the disciplining program.

Fear of law suits for action taken by peer review boards has been cited frequently as a deterrent to physicians' involvement in the disciplinary process.

It is interesting to note that the Association of American Physicians and Surgeons opposed the PSRO legislation and took legal action to prevent its implementation. These efforts, which ended in defeat when the U.S. Supreme Court refused to set aside a lower court ruling, did little to enhance the public image of the medical profession as disinterested in peer review. The doctors had contended that the legislation violated their rights to practice and the rights of their patients to receive treatment.[5]

Considering the disciplining problem from the standpoint of hospital officials it is argued that denying staff privileges, the right for a doctor to have his or her patients admitted to the hospital, has become more difficult because of changes in civil rights law and court decisions. Staff privileges are usually granted on a one-year basis only.

Some doctors, however, do not seek to place the blame for lack of discipline elsewhere. One of these is John H. Knowles, M.D., president of the Rockefeller Foundation and former head of Massachusetts General Hospital. Dr. Knowles stated:

> When I was in Massachusetts, the Medical Society was alerted to a doctor doing about 80 disc operations a year. That was as many as the Massachusetts General Hospital, with a stable of the finest orthopedic surgeons in the world, was doing. And every doctor in that doctor's community knew what he was doing, yet no one complained.
>
> It is a pox on the profession to let this kind of foolishness go

on. Medicine should root out its own incompetence and set its own standards. And it should do it now.[6]

New Jersey State Insurance Commissioner James Sheeran said "most doctors are able practitioners"; however, "their failure to take action to expel from the profession notorious incompetents marks them as accomplices in a conspiracy of inaction."[7]

In their book *The Medical Offenders* Howard and Martha Lewis observed that "laxity within the profession is only part of the larger problem of medical discipline." They said:

> Even if a repeated offender is expelled from his medical society and removed from his hospital staff, he can still legally practice medicine as long as he continues to be licensed. The chances are he will stay in practice, for nationwide the licensing of physicians is generally inadequate and ineffective as a disciplinary measure. State Legislatures almost universally have failed to draft licensing statutes that keep the unfit from practicing. State medical licensing boards do not generally pursue their disciplinary functions. . . .
>
> Throughout the country a medical license is virtually a blank check. The licensee can perform any medical or surgical service he wishes, even if they are far beyond his skills.
>
> Moreover, once a medical license is granted it is virtually permanent, subject only to the paying of a periodic fee. As a practical matter, withdrawing a physician's privilege to practice is nearly impossible for other than a felony conviction. Indeed in many states the law makes no provision for suspending a license even when it is proved that the doctor is grossly negligent, or that he exploits his patients, or even that he is mentally incapacitated.[8]

Sam Rhem, M.D., of Houston, Texas, who practiced medicine for ten years before going back to school to obtain a law degree, favors limited licensure for doctors. He said: "There are some doctors doing abdominal hysterectomies who should be directing traffic." Rhem pointed out that legally he can still practice medicine although he has been away from the field for five years.[9]

Another problem is cited by Robert C. Derbyshire, M.D., of the Federation of State Medical Boards: "The most difficult situation is presented by the disreputable physician, not a member of a medical society, or of a hospital staff, defiant of all the rules of good medical practice who perpetrates his crimes upon an unsuspecting public in the sanctuary of his office."[10]

The HEW Commission on Medical Malpractice reported:

"State Boards generally appear to be limiting themselves largely to policing cases of criminal conduct or moral turpitude rather than to monitoring the quality of practice. A change of emphasis in the interest of patient care appears to be in order."[11]

An attorney who specializes in defending doctors and hospitals said everyone needs discipline. He agrees that doctors are too protective of their peers. A doctor may be an incompetent anesthetist, for example, but his peers will not take action against him because he is a "good guy," has eight children, and is a pillar of the community. Doctors are disciplined, he claimed, only if they do not pay their dues, if they advertise, or if they fail to pay their income taxes. Another attorney emphasized that lawyers are disciplined by judges and that practicing doctors are expected to pass judgment upon practicing doctors.

Trial Lawyer President Robert Cartwright said that "out of 239,363 practicing doctors for the years 1969 to 1973, only 366 licenses were revoked and 176 suspended for that five-year period of time in the entire United States. In many states there were none." This is in contrast to figures provided by the American Bar Association which show that in a shorter span of time, four years, 1971 through 1974, a total of 1,691 attorneys resigned or were disbarred, suspended or reprimanded.[12]

The case of Dr. Nork highlighted the weaknesses of the California disciplinary system under the direction of the Board of Medical Examiners. The report of the California Assembly Select Committee on Medical Malpractice detailed some of the problems of that state's disciplining process. Many of the committee's comments can be applied to most other states. The committee said the board has a "dismal record of disciplinary proceedings on the basis of physician incompetence." It said:

> A case in point is that of Dr. John Nork, a Sacramento surgeon who for years performed needless and negligent back operations on hundreds of unwitting patients. In the past few years, the facts concerning Dr. Nork have become well known within the medical-legal community as a result of a series of lawsuits brought against him. But it was not until November 1973, after a court opinion concerning Dr. Nork and severely criticizing the Board, that disciplinary action was commenced. This evidence leads the Committee to the conclusion that the physicians on the Board—and these are 11 out of the 12 Board members—are simply opposed to an active governmental interest in a thorough investigation of the quality of health care mandated by the Medical Practice Act.[13]

The committee said the action of other groups in disciplining doctors, such as "tissue and other peer review committees . . . leave much to be desired." It also said:

> No such committee, for instance, ever took action against Dr. Nork during the long period he was practicing at a reputable hospital in Sacramento. In fact, the evidence showed that Dr. Nork has a good reputation at the hospital. It was only after his insurance was cancelled, due to a series of lawsuits, that his privileges were curtailed. The only explanation for his good reputation was that no one told anyone anything. It appears that the social and economic pressures on physicians who serve on peer review committees impair their ability to objectively evaluate the performance of their fellow doctors.
>
> County medical societies also serve as a type of peer review structure and generally have the authority to expel a doctor from membership if he is practicing incompetently. But such committees also have limited effectiveness. Not only are they subject to many of the same pressures which impair the effectiveness of hospital peer review committees, but the county society also sponsors the group insurance program for its members' protection against litigation. This problem was also raised in the Nork opinion by Judge Goldberg when he asked whether the society's "predominant interest is to defend the indefensible doctor rather than to elevate the standards of the medical profession or to protect the patients."[14]

Another example of the past ineffectiveness of peer review is a mortality survey committee of doctors in Philadelphia. During its eight years of existence the committee which was part of the Philadelphia County Medical Society reviewed "hospital deaths caused by alleged malpractice but kept no records and took no disciplinary action." Norman Kendall, M.D., head of the committee for four years, admitted that "the findings were never passed along to the state Board of Medical Education and Licensure, which controls doctors' licenses to practice." Marvin Aronson, M.D., Philadelphia medical examiner, said "the committee never disciplined doctors."[15]

The inadequacies of the New York State system came before the public in the case of Max Jacobson, M.D., a general practitioner in New York City, who had achieved fame earlier for his treatment of prominent people. The case took more than six years from beginning to end. The chronology of the case, listed below, was provided by Elliott E. Leuallen, M.D., associate commissioner for the professions in the New York State Education Department. Dr. Leuallen said:

This case was opened in our Division of Professional Conduct on April 1, 1969. Following a careful investigation, information was submitted to a Committee on Professional Conduct of the State Board for Medicine on September 16, 1970. Charges were voted on that day by the Committee and referred to the Office of the Assistant Attorney General on September 18, 1970. At the request of the Assistant Attorney General, the investigation was continued in order to establish clearly all available evidence.

The first hearing before a Committee on Professional Conduct of the State Board for Medicine was held on April 18, 1973. During the ensuing 14 months a total of 19 hearings were held. It was necessary that these hearings be scheduled at a time when the five members of the hearing panel were available as well as the respondent's attorney. A transcript of the record of each day's hearing was available to the Assistant Attorney General and the respondent's attorney following each hearing.

The hearing panel rendered a report of its findings, determination and recommendation, dated February 25, 1975. The matter was scheduled for review by the Regents Committee on Professional Discipline on March 12, 1975, but adjourned at the request of the respondent until April 11, 1975. On that date the respondent appeared in person and was represented by his attorney. The report and recommendation of the Regents' Committee was presented to the full Board of Regents and acted on by the full Board on April 25, 1975.[16]

Before revoking Dr. Jacobson's license, the Regents received a forty-two-page report which pictured the doctor's office "as a place where patients were routinely injected with heavy doses of amphetamines (speed)—where new patients received amphetamines without first being examined medically, where patients using amphetamines injected other patients and themselves and where other unpaid and unlicensed volunteers, themselves using the drug, worked in a crude laboratory mixing the drugs to be administered."[17]

Another well-publicized New York State case involving doctor discipline is that of Stewart and Cyril Marcus, twin brothers who, days after dismissal from their positions as gynecologists at New York Hospital–Cornell Medical Center, were found dead in their apartment. The New York Times reported on August 19, 1975, that the Medical Examiner's office "determined that they had been barbiturate addicts for some time and had died of the typical severe withdrawal symptoms." E. Hugh Luckey, M.D., president of the hospital, said: "There were indications that the performances of the Marcus brothers were declining and . . . they were asked to take a leave of absence and advised to seek medical care." When they returned several months later, they were placed under "special supervision" while hospital officials sought to determine if they were fit to return to practice. The final decision was a negative one. In May 1975 the Marcus brothers were told that their appointments to the hospital staff would not be renewed. Their services were terminated as of July 1.

Dr. Luckey admitted that traditional steps of disciplining doctors were not working. He said in *The New York Times* article:

> Recent articles lead one to the conclusion that we must find better ways of dealing with the competency of all individuals holding the type of precious private trust which anyone in the public service holds. Consideration of new and different mechanisms must continue in order to assure, to the extent possible, competency of anyone who has responsibility for life, liberty, or the pursuit of happiness of others.
>
> Large institutions such as the New York Hospital–Cornell Medical Center have searched for many years to find improved ways of adequate surveillance of staff members, in all categories from interns to the most senior staff, to oversee more effectively their competence, professional and otherwise, to carry out their duties.

The team approach is one technique of supervising medical personnel. Luckey said, "At no one time is there only one individual in the position of sole responsibility; there is always the participation of others—nurses, other doctors, medical students, and members of the family."

As of May 1977, attorneys for New York Hospital pointed out that no malpractice suits had been filed against the hospital or the late Marcus brothers for acts committed during the time that their health or mental condition was impaired. One suit against the brothers arose out of an incident which took place prior to the period in question.[18]

Following the Marcus brothers case, the hospital in 1976 revised its staff bylaws which now require that physicians who observe physical or mental behavior of a fellow physician which might jeopardize patients must report such to the head of the department. The new procedure involves a mandatory review and can lead to an immediate suspension of staff privileges.[19]

It was noted that the Marcus brothers were not salaried employees of the hospital and that in their last year of affiliation they had twenty-three admissions and were in the hospital for a combined total of parts of only fifty days. At a New York State Assembly hearing in 1977, testimony brought forth the fact that other physicians were sending their wives to the Marcus brothers up to the time that they were denied continuation of staff privileges. The Marcus brothers were specialists in obstetrics and gynecology with particular emphasis on problems of infertility.[20]

Kin of patients treated by them and former colleagues of the Marcus brothers described several instances when the two doctors were reportedly impaired. The husband of a patient testified that one of the brothers "arrived at the emergency room of the New York hospital three hours late, weaving and bobbing like a drunk who has just been pulled to his feet and was about to fall over again." The doctor later left the hospital and the woman was treated by other physicians.[21]

A technician said she saw Dr. Cyril Marcus perform a circumcision when he was sweating profusely and staggering, and he did not appear to have his balance. Dr. Marcus, she added, bounced off the wall and staggered while going to the mother's room after the procedure.[22]

The death of the Marcus Brothers also brought into focus the problem of the addict-doctor. Herbert C. Modlin, M.D., of the Menninger Foundation in Topeka, Kansas, said 1 to 2 percent of this country's doctors (3,000 to 6,000) are drug addicts.[23]

Richard E. Palmer, M.D., president of the American Medical Association in 1977, estimated that "about 17,000 of the 408,000 doctors—one in 24—registered nationally are impaired.[24]

Frank Chappell of the AMA, in an interview carried in the *Syracuse Herald Journal,* April 25, 1977, claimed that alcoholism and narcotics addiction in the medical profession are "higher than average because of the pressure doctors are under, dealing with life and death situations every day." Chappell said that doctors have a greater than average chance of becoming drug addicts because they have easy access to drugs.

Medical societies in the states of New York, Washington, Minnesota, Florida, and California have established programs to deal with sick physicians. In New York State, for example, doctors have been asked "to report suspected addicts among their colleagues to a confidential committee that would attempt to get the doctor off drugs and into treatment."[25]

Several years ago another peer review procedure was established by the New York State Medical Society in cooperation with its insurance carrier. The society's Professional Medical Liability Insurance and Defense Board studies individual malpractice claims to determine if the doctor should be surcharged or dropped from the insurance program.

New York doctors note that their society's board had recommended that Dr. Max Jacobson's insurance be dropped two years before the state's Board of Regents took away his license to practice. However, only ten doctors or fewer are dropped each year from the insurance program.[26]

Insufficient funding for regulatory agencies is one valid point raised by department heads in trying to explain their poor performance in the area of medical discipline. Ewald B. Nyquist, long-time New York State Education Commissioner, placed some of the blame on the state's budget-makers. He said: "In each of the last two years, the Regents have requested approximately $250,000 to strengthen the Department's investigative functions. Increased state support must be provided to assure increased service." This funding was not approved until the crisis of 1975. Nyquist noted that the department has twenty investigators responsible for 407,825 licensed and registered professionals, including 48,500 physicians. Nyquist said the number of licensed and registered professionals increased by 10 percent during the last five years, while the number of investigators decreased by 35 percent.[27]

In the five-year period ended December 31, 1974, there were sixty-eight revocations, suspensions, probations, censures, and reprimands of New York State doctors by the Board of Regents.[28] In the same five-year period a total of 274 of the approximately 60,000 attorneys in New York State were disbarred, withdrew from practice, were suspended, or censured as a result of charges made against them.[29]

The report on medical malpractice in Michigan mentioned the fact that the Medical Practice Board has "a maximum of one and one-half investigators assigned to investigate the alleged abuses of Michigan's 11,000 licensed doctors." Although the board is obviously understaffed, the report said, it spent only 34 percent of its budget in 1973–74.[30]

Emlyn I. Griffith, an attorney, who is chairman of the New York State Board of Regents Committee on Professional Discipline, said: "There are a lot of people in the professions that don't want to be open to public scrutiny, partly out of human nature and partly to maintain the mystique of the professions." Griffith admitted that most professions, including medicine, are not doing a satisfactory job of disciplining themselves in the face of increased public expectations. He attributed this to (1) human nature ("live and let live" philosophy); (2) a tendency of professionals to think that public disclosure of one incompetent reflects on the whole profession; (3) a further tendency to preserve the "mystique" of the learned professions; (4) all professionals consider themselves too busy to initiate complaints and then to testify or sit on review boards. He said the disciplinary process for doctors is extremely complicated and time consuming and involves patients, hospitals, tissue committees, utilization committees and Medicaid and Medicare bureaucrats. Griffith commented: "Doctors expect George to do it, but George doesn't do it often enough or well enough."[31]

Griffith took note of the professional resistance to licensing and discipline by laymen. He also pointed out professional resistance and a defensive attitude toward consumerism. He said that until the medical malpractice crisis hit the "pocketbook nerve" there was little motivation for doctors to come to grips with discipline.

Griffith conceded that the New York State Education Department had not kept pace with changing conditions, including the great explosion of licensed professionals which naturally led to more discipline cases. The department was hampered by an acute lack of investigative personnel. He cited the fact that the Division of Professional Misconduct had operated without a permanent director for twenty-six months.

Regarding lack of personnel, Griffith said that in 1974 the State Education Department had twenty-six investigators, twelve responsible for licensed pharmacies and registered pharmacists, and fourteen to handle the other twenty-two professions under its jurisdiction.

Practitioners and medical societies seem to do little, however, to assist the Education Department in bringing disciplinary cases to the attention of the state agency. Of 224 complaints about physicians received in 1974 by the Education Department, only eight came from physicians and two from medical societies.

Griffith said the legal profession does a better job in disciplining than does the medical profession. He admitted that there is a tradition for this because most lawyers take seriously their role as officers of the court.

Griffith suggested that a better reporting system would assist the disciplinary process for physicians and that professional societies and hospitals should have more authority to discipline. He favors mandatory continuing professional education and relicensing requirement for all professions, and in 1975 advocated that doctors should be permitted to advertise their specialties and fee ranges. This type of advertising was finally approved by the U.S. Supreme Court in 1977.

In the summer of 1977 the New York State Board of Regents adopted a three-part package which Regent Griffith said was aimed at improving the quality of professional services throughout the state. The new regulations permitted doctors to advertise for the first time since 1923, when the Regents banned price advertising in the health field.[32]

Griffith said: "They must have a system for telling consumers what they can do and what they intend to charge. Many malpractice claims involve someone trying to do something that he isn't qualified to do or patients or clients dissatisfied with the results in relation to the fees charged."[33] Griffith repeated the expression that "self-discipline is a free man's yoke" and urged general improvement of existing disciplinary processes in order to serve the public interest and to prevent ultimate socialization of the professions.

Looking ahead, some observers, such as the authors of the Michigan Report, said that "one side effect of the deep concern over the malpractice problem has been the realization that the regulation of the capabilities of doctors is virtually non-existent."[34]

The California Assembly Select Committee on Medical Malpractice said: "By generating interest and concern over the problems of our existing mechanisms of quality control, the malpractice controversy is not only benefiting the public, but may contribute to solutions which will further elevate the integrity of the health care profession."[35]

In addressing the malpractice issue, many state legislatures streamlined, revised and restructured the disciplining process. To be successful, however, the new mechanisms will need the full support of health care providers as well as all segments of the public.

James H. Sammons, M.D., executive vice-president of the American Medical Association, said that doctors must by their actions prove their willingness to be part of the disciplining process. In testimony before a congressional committee, Dr. Sammons said: "Only when physicians report violations . . . and are willing to testify if needed, can the medical profession demonstrate to the public that the profession is fulfilling its responsibilities."[36]

Postscript to the Secretary's Commission on Medical Malpractice

W HEN MEDICAL MALPRACTICE became front-page news in 1974 and 1975, the only multistate and multidiscipline study of the issue up to that time was that of the U.S. Secretary of Health, Education and Welfare's Commission. The report of the commission was a primer on the subject for legislators and others.

The commission began its work in September of 1971 and issued its final report on January 16, 1973. In terms of time, talent, efforts, and funds expended, the commission's contributions were monumental.

The group conducted seven public hearings throughout the country and heard from 212 witnesses, "103 representing health care interests, 16 representing insurance interests, 25 representing legal interests and 68 representing the general public."[1] The testimony is recorded on 3,568 pages of transcript and will be cited extensively in this chapter. The recommendations of the commission are contained in its 146-page report which had a companion appendix of 870 pages summarizing eleven research studies financed by the commission (see Appendix D).

Although some place the cost of the HEW Commission study at $2 million or more, Eli P. Bernzweig, executive director of the commission, claimed expenditures were actually $1.3 million. He said: "As a matter of fact, the Commission turned money back to the federal treasury because there wasn't really time to do all the studies that the money would have been helpful to do."[2]

From the outset the commission's activities were surrounded by controversy, as has been the case ever since with any heterogeneous group seeking to deal with the malpractice issue.

Richard M. Markus, a Cleveland, Ohio, attorney and a member of the commission, recalled that the composition of the commission was criticized by the news media as having "too many foxes and not enough chickens." Markus pointed out that "approximately three-quarters of the 21-member commission were health care providers, malpractice insurance executives, or lawyers who regularly represent the providers or their insurers. Although 12 members of the commission hold law degrees, only one has experience in representing patients in professional liability cases."[3]

Roger O. Egeberg, M.D., assistant secretary of Health, Education and Welfare at the time, explained the selection process for the commission:

> Secretary Richardson and I picked what we thought was a very good commission, and sent it in, but we got the word from the White House Committee on Commissions that wasn't the way you did it. You sent in 40 names and they picked the 16 or 17 they thought should be on it. We thought of 40 people that we would be delighted to see on it, but while we had a balanced commission, the one they gave us had 10 lawyers and 4 doctors, and 2 of them were also lawyers. With lawyers, the doctors are at a disadvantage at 1 to 1, so when they found themselves at 4 to 10, they really felt miffed, and came out with somewhat of a different report, at least their exceptions made up 30 pages.[4]

According to Markus, the doctors got help from the legal staff of the American Medical Association which assigned a staff person to attend commission meetings. Markus said: "The American Medical Association staff member tried to persuade commissioners themselves and even prepared language for submission as part of the commission report through one of the commissioners."[5]

As the commission was completing its work, several members felt they needed additional time before issuing the final report. Commission member Howard Hassard had asked HEW Secretary Elliot L. Richardson for permission for an additional meeting of the Commission on Medical Malpractice to review further its draft report before submission on January 17. Richardson denied the request.

The report included a separate statement by Hassard, concurred in by seven other commission members, citing his reasons for the need for the additional meeting. Hassard said:

> The Commissioners received from staff the "Draft Final Report of the Secretary's Commission on Medical Malpractice," dated January 5, 1973, between January 8 and 10, 1973. The Secretary's telegram points out that the report was required to be submit-

ted to him on January 17, 1973. The Commissioners, all of whom have other obligations, were thus given less than a week to study and react to the entire report.

I am unaware of any deadline or of any factor that necessitates a report in January 1973 as against February and March of 1973. True, the medical profession and all others in the health field, as well as the general public, desire solutions to problems existing in the medical malpractice field, but I am certain that everyone concerned would prefer a thoroughly studied document to one rushed through to meet an unexplainable hurried deadline.

In my opinion, the members of the Commission were given an inadequate period of time to review, study and propose improvements to the official report and were, unfortunately, denied an opportunity to meet together and through comparison with each other's reactions develop a true "Commission" report. There is no certainty, of course, that further time would have improved the report, but those of us who served on the Commission will, I believe, continue to feel that we were given short shrift.[6]

Another committee member, James Ludlam, a California attorney, took the plea to H. R. Haldeman. Ludlam said the commission members "were willing to meet at their own time and at their own expense, in order to have extra time to review the final draft of the report as well as the bulk of the research that we received after the report was drafted." Haldeman turned Ludlam down.[7]

All of the recommendations, it should be noted, were voted upon by the commission during its meetings which preceded the writing of the final report.

The report provided the first extensive statistics on malpractice. The commission studied closed claims files for the year 1970, when 16,000 claims files were closed. Of that total, 50 percent were closed without a lawsuit, with some payment in about 25 percent of the cases closed without legal action. "The rest of the claims that did not become lawsuits were abandoned or settled without any payment to the claimant."

Of those claims closed in 1970 which resulted in lawsuits, 80 percent never went to trial. Twenty percent of the cases that did not go to trial produced payment. Of the cases that went to trial, the defendant won 80 percent of the verdicts.

Considering all 16,000 claims closed in 1970, "there was payment in approximately 45 percent of all claims, whether or not a lawsuit was filed." Insurance carriers were asked to pass upon the merits of the closed claims on the basis of whether or not it was "legally meritorious in terms of liability." Forty-six percent of the claims were called meritorious by the insurance companies.

The report showed that of claims paid, 59.5 percent received less than $3,000. Only 6.1 percent exceeded $40,000. The commission said, however, that there is little doubt that the number of awards, or settlements, has been increasing dramatically within the recent past.

The commission's profile of alleged injuries for claims files closed in 1970 showed that of 12,000 claimed injuries "19 percent left permanent effects and 18 percent resulted in death. At the other extreme, 12 percent of the alleged injuries were primarily psychological. Excluding patients who died, two-thirds of the alleged injuries were temporary in nature."

On the question of defensive medicine, "The Commission finds that defensive medicine is practiced, but the extent to which it is practiced is not known. It does increase the cost of medical care, but it is doubtful that this increased cost is measurable."

The commission recognized the economic impact of medical malpractice: "While inflation is the primary cause of rising medical care costs (accounting for 47 percent of the increase) with population growth accounting for another 17 percent, among the other forces accounting for the remaining 36 percent are the costs of malpractice claims and suits. Medical malpractice clearly has increased the cost of medical care."

Debate among commission members concerning legal issues pertaining to malpractice was heated and opinion was fairly evenly divided. In his statement, included in the report, Dr. Monroe Trout, one of the two commission members who is both a medical doctor and an attorney, said:

> The Commission defeated by a single vote margin a motion that stated, "The Commission recognizes that some courts abuse legal doctrines such as informed consent, res ipsa loquitur, the discovery rule, and oral guarantees, to find strict liability in medical malpractice cases where negligence was not a factor and recommends that state legislatures take remedial action where such abuses of legal doctrines have occurred." After this motion was defeated, a substitute motion was introduced and passed by a two vote margin.

Following are some of the conclusions reached by the commission in the legal area:

The Commission finds that the doctrine of res ipsa loquitur in its classical sense performs a useful purpose in common law, but that it should not be applied differently in medical malpractice cases than in other types of tort litigation. . . .

The Commission finds that the doctrine of informed consent is subject to abuse when it imposes an unreasonable responsibility upon the physician. . . .

The Commission finds that some courts have applied certain legal doctrines for the purpose of creating or relieving the liability of health professionals. The Commission further finds that such special doctrines, or the application thereof, are no longer justified.

The Commission recommends that legal doctrines relating to the liability of health professionals should be applied in the same manner as they are applied to all classes of defendants, whether they be favorable or unfavorable to health professional defendants. Such doctrines would include (a) the application of the discovery rule under the statute of limitations; (b) the terms of the statute of limitations; (c) the application of the doctrine of res ipsa loquitur to injuries arising in the performance of professional services; (d) the rule allowing liability based on oral guarantee of good results, and (e) the doctrine of informed consent to treatment.

The contingent legal fee came under close scrutiny by the commission, which recommended that state legislatures establish "a uniform graduated scale of contingent fee rates in all medical malpractice litigation. The contingent fee scale should be one in which the fee rate decreases as the recovery amount increases."

The Commission made the following comments on legal fees:

The Commission finds that the contingent fee arrangement discourages the acceptance of meritorious low-recovery cases. The Commission further finds that on a fee-for-service basis, potential clients would be similarly discouraged from pursuing these same meritorious low-recovery cases, since the average citizen cannot financially support the required lawyer's services. . . .

The Commission finds that by analytically reducing average plaintiff lawyers' contingent fees to an hourly basis for comparison purposes, there does not appear to be any gross discrepancy between the resultant rates charged by the plaintiff bar and those charged by the defense bar in medical malpractice cases.

The hourly fee for plaintiff lawyers came to an average of $63 as compared with $50 for defense lawyers.

"The Commission finds that when, under the contingent fee

arrangement, a plaintiff attorney loses a case he will have invested a considerable amount of uncompensated time on that case." A study by the commission showed that the average number of plaintiff-lawyer hours spent on zero recovery litigated cases was 440 hours per case.

The commission proposed elimination of ad damnum clauses in malpractice suits which place a dollar amount on the malpractice claim:

> It is the opinion of the Commission that the astronomical amounts of damages set forth in malpractice complaints by attorneys are an unnecessary source of friction between the legal and medical professions. These large demands attract sensational newspaper coverage, impose needless anxiety and often unfounded notoriety upon defendant physicians, create a feeling of unfair persecution in the medical world and are of no special benefit to plaintiff-patients.

Establishment of a nationwide data-gathering and information system was perhaps one of the most significant recommendations in the report, but as noted in Chapter 1, it went unheeded until a crisis in availability of insurance occurred in late 1974 and 1975.

Greater consumer involvement in health care decision-making was proposed by the commission. Consumerism, despite its many benefits also poses many problems.

Commission member George W. Northup, M.D., said in the report:

> Consumerism is a magic word in contemporary society. No one knowingly wants to offend the consumer, but consumerism as a viable movement sometimes defies precise definition. Who does the consumer representative represent? All consumers? The poor or near poor? Ethnic groups? And so the list can go.
>
> Many of us believe in the principle of consumer representation, but who selects the consumer representation and from which groups? What does one look for in a good consumer representative? What should our methodology of selection be? If there are bad doctors, bad lawyers, bad insurance companies, are there not bad consumers? Society should be protected against bad professionals, but should it not also be protected against bad consumers, as well?

In its chapter on prevention of unnecessary claims, the commission stated: "Many patients are moved to litigate because they are dissatisfied with the outcome of medical treatment and have been frustrated in their efforts to obtain either explanations, advice or even a sympathetic ear, much less redress." The commission,

commission has been a number of information meetings. If some of the recommendations of the commission had been implemented, he said, we would at least have gathered some data by now which would be helpful in plotting future action. Bernzweig said the federal government's failure to act is due in no small part to the medical profession's opposition to the report. He recalled that one of the doctor members of the commission became incensed during a commission meeting and insisted that the quality of care has nothing to do with the malpractice problem.

Roger Egeberg, M.D., assistant secretary of HEW, had the following explanation for the federal government's failure to act on the commission's recommendations:

> The report has a lot of very good information in it which had not been brought together in one place before, but it did say that malpractice is not federal business, and it also said that there was no crisis. They didn't see one coming. All right, if there was no crisis and we had said, "Well, it may not be federal business, but let's do something about it," I wonder how many people we could have gotten to listen to us. It wasn't easy to get people aroused at that particular time.
>
> My feeling is that the time has come to get something done about the malpractice situation, and it had not come a couple of years ago.
>
> Now the issue, as I'm sure you've been told many times, is certainly complex and it is a State problem and the only excuse we can give for coming into it is that we have patients in all the States, and should it get to an impasse in any one State where there was no insurance available, and the doctors couldn't practice, it would be our business. Also, it's becoming our business in a gradual way in inhibiting doctors from practicing in certain areas, and in making older people as they start to retire, retire suddenly rather than gradually. I know of three, no it's now four or five friends, who had intended to gradually taper off their practice over a period of five or six years.They would have been happier, and I'm sure their patients would have been happier, but they stopped on the anniversary of their malpractice insurance.[8]

It is interesting to note some years later the reactions of commission members to subsequent events concerning medical malpractice. Their thoughts were as varied as they were during the commission's deliberations.

Wendell G. Freeland, a Pittsburgh attorney who was chairman of the commission, feels that its recommendations are even more valid today than they were in 1973. He said that the malpractice problem must be tackled in bits and pieces as there is no simple, easy solution. In his opinion, some of the legislative responses have been irrational and purely political. However, in many instances, he said, legislative proposals have been developed with a sincere intent to help alleviate the problem.

Freeland opposes placing limits on awards and any efforts to have the states assume a portion of the cost in "disaster cases." He said a limit on the contingency fee is desirable but tort law changes will probably not have any great effect in reducing the frequency and severity of malpractice claims.

The commission chairman said the major reason for malpractice claims is negligence. The quality of health care, he added, must improve and there is a need to experiment in the next five years to determine who pays the cost of such, including the cost related to medical malpractice fears and claims.

In the long run, Freeland commented, institutions will become responsible for the quality of care and the onus will shift from the individual physician. The institutions, he said, must develop greater controls, and insurance companies must develop accident prevention procedures similar to those used by workmen's compensation carriers.[9]

Dr. Hoffman, a commission member and past president of the AMA, stated that the malpractice situation has changed drastically since the HEW Commission report was published in 1973. He claimed that an abundance of critical problems have surfaced and that if the report were made today it would probably be different. Dr. Hoffman admitted he was surprised by the explosion of the malpractice problem, which he attributes to five primary factors: (1) people becoming more liability conscious; (2) inflation; (3) the activity of trial lawyers; (4) the legislative climate; and (5) a weakening of the doctor-patient relationship. With subsequent legislation enactments he is hopeful but not optimistic. He is anxious to see the federal government stay out of the picture and let the states deal with the problem on an individual basis.[10]

James E. Ludlam, in his dissenting statement in the HEW report, said the solution to the problem does not lie with government or with the insurance industry but with committed leadership by health care providers. He states that new mechanisms for compensation must be developed. An attempt to solve the problem under the tort adversary system is not in accordance with modern trends of injury compensation. It should be based, Ludlam said, upon a sharing of responsibility on a broad base such as through health insurance, not the individual liability of the physician.

Regarding his later views, Ludlam, who has worked closely with hospitals, commented that his 1973 statement was not nearly strong enough. He still views malpractice as a social issue. It is becoming clear, he said, that the ability to fund the system is now beyond the scope of the health care provider.

Ludlam has been active in setting up an arbitration system in California hospitals. The plan, which involved less than a dozen hospitals at the outset, has now grown to include more than three dozen hospitals. He said the plan has been sabotaged by all parties and there are so few cases of arbitration they can draw no broad conclusions as to an impact on rates except that all indications are that arbitration will encourage settlements and decrease the cost of claims handling.[11]

Another commission member, Esther Schiff, a practicing attorney in Miami Beach, Florida, was subsequently involved in efforts to institute a voluntary binding arbitration plan in Florida. She encountered the same kind of difficulties that Ludlam experienced in California. The parties involved in arbitration were unwilling to cooperate. She said lawyers were worried about their fees and the plaintiffs and physicians were doing their best to scuttle the plan.

Mrs. Schiff said that what constitutes a compensable injury must be determined through a definition. If a compensable injury, irrespective of negligence, could be defined, she said, a no-fault system might be developed as an alternative method of payment. She noted that government plays an important role in regulating as well as financing a substantial portion of payment for medical care. The federal government plays an effective role in not only eliciting facts about the malpractice problem but also in initiating measures to resolve it.[12]

Monroe Trout, M.D., an executive of Sterling Drug, Inc., of New York, said:

> Many of the hard decisions that need to be made cannot be made at this time because of lack of data. Hopefully that situation will be corrected in the next year or two. Also, I think it should be kept in mind that any law which is passed will not have any major impact for three to five years. In addition, I doubt whether any law will have any impact at this time on the root cause of malpractice (i.e., the one to five million estimated medical injuries which occur each year

in the United States). It was estimated by our Commission that 20 per cent of these were due to negligence. This part of the problem will only be solved when we know the universe and can provide educational programs for prevention.

It is also important to remember that the malpractice problem will never be solved completely. There will always be careless or incompetent physicians, but with new legislation being passed in most of the states in regard to licensure this part of the problem should be able to be kept at a minimal level.[13]

Trout proposed a limitation on the number of defendants in a malpractice suit. He continued: "At the present time complaints cover the waterfront and in many cases are the result of poor homework on the part of the attorney. For each defendant there must be a defense and this, of course, increases costs. Fishing expeditions, however, should not be permitted and there should be consideration of a penalty for such."

Richard M. Markus, a member of the American Bar Association's Commission on Medical Professional Liability and the Association of Trial Lawyers Professional Legislative Committee, said the most recent legislative enactments take the position that a restriction on the claimant's right to recover would reduce malpractice costs, which Markus said is an erroneous assumption.

Markus believes that extremes in insurance rates are not justified with one physician paying up to ten times the amount in premiums as another. If a physician is to share in the bounty of the system, he said, the physician should share in the risk by paying part of the total premium on an equal basis.

He said although there has been an increase in the frequency of malpractice claims, such increases are not as large as some individuals or groups allege. Markus pointed out that the American Bar Association is considering various proposals, including the system in which the hospital pays the malpractice premium for everyone who works there. He felt that this procedure, called channeling, would help to cut costs substantially since the hospital would be legally liable and any insurance claim filed involving the hospital would have only one defendant. He maintains that this and other economic solutions to the economic problem merit more attention than attempts to tinker with the patient's right to payment.[14]

Public reaction to the commission and its report, like opinion within the commission itself, was mixed. While some claim that the commission offered no concrete solutions to the malpractice issue after expenditures of a large sum of money, others use the commission report as a bible, quoting from it to support their arguments on this complex subject.

Although some of the findings and recommendations were controversial, it must be stated that the commission offered the country much food for thought. It is most unfortunate that the delay between thought and action was so prolonged.

·◦[7]◦··

New York State's Response

THE NEW YORK STATE LEGISLATURE'S WORK with the malpractice issue
dates back to 1970, the year that the American Osteopathic Association and the U.S. Department of Health, Education and Welfare, sponsored what was billed as the First National Conference on
Medical Malpractice.

Recognizing the growing importance of all aspects of the
medical malpractice problem on the health care delivery system,
State Senator Norman F. Lent, chairman of the Senate Health Committee, scheduled a public hearing on the subject for September 28,
1970, in New York City. Speakers were asked to consider four areas.
They were:

1. Whether a statutory distinction can or should be drawn
between gross or unquestionable acts of negligence and cases involving questions of medical judgment.

2. Whether some other system of compensation to the injured
patient should be devised such as compulsory arbitration or establishment of fixed indemnities as in Workmen's Compensation.

3. Whether notice of claim should be required within 90 days
of discovery of alleged malpractice as a condition precedent to suit.

4. Proposals for improving training and updating skills of
health professionals and paramedical personnel.[1]

These topics and Senator Lent's opening remarks at the hearing are just as relevant today as they were in 1970:

> What we have is a breakdown in the relationship between
> doctor and patient, between institution and patient, reflecting per-
> haps the impersonal character of medicine as it is practiced today by
> busy specialists, overworked general practitioners and understaffed
> institutions.

83

The danger lies in the fact that the practice of medicine may be inhibited by the threat of malpractice suits, limiting initiative and dictating more hospitalized care and lengthy testing is not always necessary for diagnosis and cure.

A byproduct is the exorbitant cost of malpractice insurance which has risen sharply in recent years and makes its greatest impact upon our nonprofit institutions.

Today we examine this problem to determine whether legislative change in forum, trial practice, rules of evidence, or law of damages is required and advisable.

We shall also reach the question of whether the quality of medical care has disintegrated to the point where most of these suits are justified and, if so, what remedy can be pursued.

When Senator Lent was elected to Congress less than two months after that hearing, the author, who had served as a member of the committee, was appointed chairman. As a continuation of the committee's study of the malpractice issue, a conference was held in Albany on August 26, 1971, in the hopes that some concrete suggestions would be brought forth. Those in attendance were insurance company representatives and their attorneys, plaintiffs' attorneys, the president of the State Medical Society, representatives of the State Hospital Association, and the state's Departments of Education, Health, and Insurance, and the governor's office.

The conferees acknowledged that a major problem existed and that the problem was becoming increasingly critical. They could not agree on action to be taken toward workable solutions. The doctors and the insurance companies did not like the suggestions brought forth by the plaintiffs' attorneys, and the attorneys objected to suggestions made by the medical profession. The confusion of semantics, emphasis, definitions, and diversified viewpoints further complicated efforts to cope with the problem, as did the indifference to the issue of most legislators and the news media.

A dire lack of statistical data on malpractice was readily apparent and prompted the Senate Health Committee in 1971 to recommend passage of legislation mandating that insurance carriers submit detailed reports to the insurance department on all malpractice claims filed against its New York State policyholders. Doctors opposed the measure because they wanted to retain confidentiality of these records, and the insurance carriers sought to block the bill's passage because in their opinion the reports were not necessary.

The Health Committee was convinced that the subject of malpractice in New York State merited more attention and applied for a research grant from the U.S. Department of Health, Education and Welfare. The request was turned down and the department subsequently established the Secretary's Commission on Medical Malpractice. The author testified at a February 25, 1972, public hearing of the commission in New York City (see Appendix E).

The State Medical Society's dependence on one carrier (Employers Insurance of Wausau) was of grave concern to many. The author suggested that a State Insurance Fund be established to guarantee the availability of medical malpractice insurance. The proposal was rejected by representatives of the Medical Society and Employers. It was alleged that the Medical Society wanted to maintain control over the availability of insurance coverage since it used lower group insurance rates as an incentive to attract and keep its members.

In 1973, when the Medical Society was forced to look for another carrier, the author proposed to the Medical Society that it form a doctors'-owned insurance company. All of the above proposals and recommendations went unheeded until the crisis of 1975.

The only notable legislative progress prior to the crisis came in 1974 when the legislature and then Governor Malcolm Wilson approved the creation of pretrial screening and mediation panels for medical malpractice suits in the state.[2] This law became effective on September 1, 1974. These non-binding panels consist of impartial physicians, attorneys, and jurists serving on a voluntary basis. The panel system was patterned after the Stevens Mediation Panel, established in New York County in 1971 by Justice Harold A. Stevens. The Stevens Panel had disposed of 30 percent of all the cases brought before it, thus relieving the crowded malpractice calendar in New York County.

Establishment of the panels was only a small measure. Other areas proved more difficult.

While the state legislature took little action, awards on malpractice cases were increasing at an alarming rate. According to State Medical Society figures, in 1958 some $1.3 million in awards was paid out in New York by its carrier, Employers Insurance of Wausau. In 1964, this amount had increased to $2 million. In 1973, the total award figure had escalated to $17.4 million, and by the end of 1975 payments reached $28 million.

On October 3, 1973, Employers notified the State Medical

Society that it intended to terminate its insurance program with the Society. Raymond H. Bohl, vice-president for the Special Accounts Division of Employers, outlined the reasons for the withdrawal at an October 4, 1974, public hearing conducted by the legislature's Select Committee on Insurance and the Senate Health Committee. Bohl said:

> This decision was made reluctantly, and only after thorough analysis of all factors. As the record will indicate, the long history of unprofitability was not the only consideration. At least equally important was the fact that the exposure is so concentrated, and has grown so large, as to have become disproportionate to the total company "book of business." The potential liability of suits then filed represented a dollar amount of over 10 percent of company assets. [Employers of Wausau's assets currently exceed $1 billion.] The problem was compounded by the enormous inflation of verdicts and suit costs.[3]

Table 10 gives details of the carrier's experience from 1959 through 1974.

Employers' decision to withdraw from New York State came a few months after Professional Insurance Company of New York was declared insolvent. Professional "serviced approximately 15 per cent of the New York medical malpractice insurance market."[4]

In the spring of 1974, it appeared that the Medical Society might not be successful in attempts to find a new carrier. The State Insurance Department and the chairmen of the legislature's insurance committees, Senator John Dunne and Assemblyman John G. McCarthy drew up standby legislation which would have established a Joint Underwriting Association. The association, comprised of insurers writing personal injury liability insurance, would have provided malpractice protection for doctors unable to find coverage elsewhere.

Projections of the rates for the Joint Underwriting Association ranged from 200 to 300 percent more than doctors had been paying with Employers. The JUA approach was abandoned when Argonaut agreed to assume coverage for the Medical Society as of July 1, 1974, at an increase of 93 percent. Employers, which had originally proposed ending its contract as of April 1, 1974, "agreed to postpone termination of its contract with the Society to July 1 (1974)."[5]

At the October 4, 1974, hearing, Eli Bernzweig, who had left government service to become a vice-president at Argonaut, was asked if for the coming year he envisioned a premium increase similar to the 93.5 percent increase the company received when it assumed coverage for the Medical Society. Bernzweig answered: "I don't envision anything for the next year, it is too far away, but if nothing else in the world happens but just normal inflationary rises, I would say that it is a possibility that there would be some increase, but I can't say at this point in time. I don't think anybody can."[6]

The internal shakeup within Argonaut and reassessment of its vast malpractice business by its parent company Teledyne, described in Chapter 1, changed the outlook in a hurry. Among other problems, Argonaut was experiencing great difficulty in obtaining reinsurance. Argonaut President Lawrence Baker, Jr., later told a congressional subcommittee that the company had expected to reinsure 85 percent of the risk in New York.[7] New York State Insurance Department officials said the firm was successful in reinsuring only about 50 percent of the risk.

A few weeks after the October 4, 1974, public hearing, Argonaut asked the Insurance Department for permission to write malpractice policies in the state on a claims made basis. After this request was turned down, the company, on December 16, 1974, demanded a 196.8 percent increase. This announcement brought immediate massive protests from doctors and medical societies and presented the state legislature and state government with a malpractice crisis which it could no longer afford to ignore.

Immediate action was called for.

On December 27, 1974, Superintendent Benjamin Schenck, in an unprecedented move, suspended the rate increase and directed Argonaut's top officials to appear at a public hearing scheduled for January 9, 1975. This hearing was never held.

Instead, when Superintendent Schenck appeared at a joint hearing of the Senate Health and Insurance Committees on January 6, 1975, he announced that an agreement had been reached with Argonaut to continue its contract until June 30, 1975, with no increase in rates. He also reported that the company would neither renew nor renegotiate its contract with the Medical Society. The issue, which previously had been of concern only to doctors, lawyers, and insurance companies, suddenly emerged as a matter of prime importance to virtually every resident of the state.

Malpractice was one of many major problems thrust upon Hugh L. Carey when he became governor on January 1. In the November 1974 elections Carey, a Congressman from Brooklyn for

Table 10

NEW YORK MEDICAL SOCIETY

Summary of Experience

As of 12/31/75

Policy Year	Number Doctors	Earned Premium	Indemnity Losses		Allocated Loss Expense	
			Paid	Outstanding	Paid	Outstand
1959	12,474	2,442,205	2,167,962	346,087	496,661	51,9
1960	14,492	2,895,274	3,218,055	194,913	633,878	29,2
1961	15,402	3,269,021	3,983,010	640,000	671,775	96,0
1962	16,004	3,790,189	3,967,681	377,867	666,999	56,6
1963	16,731	4,121,291	4,788,370	856,965	799,149	128,5
1964	17,084	4,324,575	6,632,609	952,303	991,515	142,8
1965	17,959	4,428,084	7,322,221	1,718,989	1,120,505	195,7
1966	18,414	5,003,960	8,493,586	2,083,235	1,131,959	182,6
1967	18,236	5,906,181	10,415,769	2,513,481	1,276,209	231,1
1968	20,534	8,947,734	12,689,538	6,367,762	1,539,655	548,4
1969	21,731	11,938,608	15,059,790	11,392,104	1,973,012	1,148,7
1970	21,665	18,963,586	12,715,582	17,292,727	2,221,595	1,653,6
1971	21,238	33,256,331	9,860,564	22,548,276	2,142,559	2,243,8
1972	20,785	38,759,856	4,642,946	24,851,553	1,542,422	2,648,6
1973	20,502	36,902,906	1,014,014	25,752,745	646,899	3,354,4
1974	10,685	18,593,579	321,118	7,204,845	66,316	1,034,9

Source: Data provided by New York State Medical Society, Lake Success, New York, to New York State Sen
Health Committee, Albany, New York, 1976.

fourteen years, became the state's first Democratic governor since Averell Harriman, who had been defeated by Nelson Rockefeller in 1958. The elections also saw Democrats regain control of the State Assembly after six years of Republican control. Republicans did manage to maintain their majority in the State Senate.

In his first message to the state legislature at its opening session on January 8, Governor Carey said he was "directing the Health and Insurance Departments to report to me on a plan for controlling the absurd increases in the price of medical malpractice insurance."[8] The following week, approximately a thousand doctors converged on the State Capitol in Albany demanding action on the malpractice issue.

The State Senate was the first to act. On January 29, 1975, it approved creation of a Joint Underwriting Association (JUA) as an

otal Loss nd Alloc. xcl. IBNR	IBNR Incl. Alloc.	Number of Claims			Expenses Excl. Alloc. Loss Exp.
		Reported	Closed	Outstanding	
,062,623	0	778	770	8	544,000
,076,083	0	975	965	10	642,000
,390,785	0	1,072	1,061	11	610,000
,069,227	0	1,116	1,102	14	655,000
,573,029	0	1,177	1,153	24	671,000
,719,273	0	1,315	1,275	40	700,000
,357,473	0	1,386	1,324	62	701,000
,891,419	273,000	1,437	1,340	97	769,000
,436,604	816,000	1,423	1,269	154	910,000
,145,376	897,000	1,874	1,563	311	1,359,000
,573,705	1,226,000	2,143	1,669	474	1,657,000
,883,548	2,654,000	2,270	1,562	708	2,297,000
,795,223	3,701,000	2,170	1,255	915	3,060,000
,685,583	11,001,000	2,160	1,040	1,120	3,989,000
,768,083	21,765,000	1,966	807	1,159	4,157,000
,627,179	22,271,000	815	339	476	3,524,000

emergency measure to assure the availability of coverage necessary to preserve continuation of the state's health care delivery system. The Democrat-controlled Assembly balked at the JUA approach, and instead scheduled a series of statewide hearings.

Behind the scenes, bipartisan negotiations were under way in an attempt to reach a solution acceptable to both the senate and the assembly. These negotiations were initiated by the author and Senator John Dunne, Senate Insurance Committee Chairman, after he and Senate Majority Leader Warren M. Anderson agreed that the issue should remain above partisan politics. Daily meetings were devoted to efforts to draft legislation not only to solve the problem, but which could gain enough support to be passed by the legislature and signed into law by the governor.

It was fortunate that one of the governor's closest advisers was Kevin Cahill, M.D., a Manhattan physician who had an understanding of the problem both from a professional and political viewpoint. Dr. Cahill believed that "the medical profession has tended to remain aloof from the strife of political decision-making." He said: "The physician has a privileged position from which to view this scene but, alone, is almost impotent in effecting any change. For too long, medical professionals have spoken only to one another. . . . Too rarely has the competent respected health expert been willing to venture from our safe havens into the turbulent councils where government priorities are made and financial allocations set."[9]

The malpractice issue in the state affected hospitals as seriously as it did doctors. On February 27, 1975, Argonaut notified twenty-three of its sixty-three insured hospitals that as of March 15, rates would be increased, and the hospitals were warned that if they refused to accept the increase, policies would be cancelled.

According to the Hospital Association of New York State, the proposed increases would have added an additional $50 to each patient's bill for an average hospital stay of seven to ten days. An agreement was reached, however, between the insurance company and the State Insurance Department, which stipulated that coverage would not be cancelled before June 1, 1975. This meant that whatever action the legislature took must protect hospitals as well as doctors in the state.

On March 19, after more than two months of concentrated effort, details of a bill were made public by the governor and those legislators who had participated in the negotiations. This proposal provided for a transfer of medical disciplinary proceedings from the Board of Regents in the State Education Department to the Department of Health, reduction in the Statute of Limitations from three to two years and to ten years in the case of infants. Other provisions included abolition of the doctrine of res ipsa loquitur, the use of information on collateral source (funds the plaintiff may have received from health insurance or other third-party payments) as evidence in a malpractice trial, and use of the New York State Insurance Fund as a carrier of malpractice insurance in the event that private carriers refuse to provide adequate coverage at reasonable rates. Adequacy of coverage and reasonableness of rates are to be determined by the Superintendent of Insurance.

Although this bill (Senate 5007), was ready to be voted on prior to the Easter-Passover recess, legislative action was delayed at the request of assembly leaders and the governor's office. Opposition to various parts of the bill developed during the two-week recess.

The medical profession was vehemently opposed to use of the state fund and viewed it as another step toward socialized medicine and further governmental intervention into the practice of medicine. The insurance industry, which earlier had fought the Joint Underwriting Association concept, reversed itself and gave its support to the JUA. Insurance companies feared that government's entry into the malpractice insurance field would be a forerunner of more governmental activity in insurance.

The transfer of the disciplining of doctors from the Board of Regents to the Department of Health also became highly controversial. The State Education Commissioner and the Board of Regents were openly and effectively lobbying against the transfer. At the same time, trial lawyers were vocal in their opposition to reducing the statute of limitations and to abolishing the doctrine of res ipsa loquitur. Abolishing the doctrine was a major objective of the State Medical Society, which had inaugurated a massive advertising and public relations campaign to gain support for its stand on malpractice legislation.

The campaign, including full-page advertisements and radio commercials, was funded by an assessment of $100 on each of the 27,000 members of the State Medical Society. Failure to pay the assessment would be tantamount to withdrawal from the Medical Society. More than 97 percent of the members paid, according to Ralph S. Emerson, M.D., State Medical Society president.

Members of the Medical Society displayed posters in their offices with the heading: "To my patients: I may have to discontinue practice on July 1 this year." The poster further stated to the patient that his doctor may have to discontinue practice unless the state legislature takes corrective action. The patients were urged to write their legislators.

The campaign was effective in generating a concern among the residents of the state who, in turn, sent a large volume of mail to their state legislators. The author's mail on the subject numbered well over 10,000 cards and letters. Less than a hundred opposed legislative proposals concerning medical malpractice.

The Medical Society was seeking passage of eight of the bills in a nine-bill package (Senate Bills 4780 to 4788) which the author introduced as alternatives to the consensus bill (Senate Bill 5007) discussed earlier. Among the proposals included in this package was the creation of a Medical Injury Liability Board providing for mandatory arbitration of all malpractice claims against physicians and hospitals with the ultimate right to a jury trial. Other bills provided for admissibility into evidence at a jury trial of unanimous recommendations of mediation panels, a schedule of fees for attorneys in malpractice cases, and a constitutional amendment to permit the waiving of the right to a jury trial in malpractice cases.

Meanwhile, the bipartisan negotiations to meet the objections of the consensus bill continued and seemed headed to a successful conclusion. Invaluable in working out differences among the governor's office, the senate and the assembly was Lawrence Keepnews, who became Superintendent of Insurance in January. His death in late April represented a key loss of a valuable liaison person who had been helping advance the bipartisan efforts.

While legislative negotiations were stalemated, the State Medical Society's House of Delegates on April 28 endorsed a proposal to create the society's own insurance company. At the same time, the doctors warned that unless the legislature took positive action on the malpractice issue they would provide only emergency care after July 1 and that nonessential treatment would be phased out during June.

With negotiations at a standstill, senate leaders decided to act unilaterally in an attempt to spur the assembly into action. Three separate bills were prepared (Senate Bills 5675, 5676, and 5677). Senate Bill 5676 provided insurance coverage through a Joint Underwriting Association and a number of tort law changes. Senate Bill 5677 would allow the recommendations of mediation panels to be read to a jury, and Senate Bill 5675 would transfer the disciplinary proceedings from the Board of Regents to the Health Department.

The insurance bill and the mediation panel bill were approved with strong bipartisan support. The discipline bill was not considered.

Lengthy debate on the bills covered the gamut of opinion on the entire malpractice issue.

Senate Minority Leader Manfred Ohrenstein of New York City expressed criticism of the medical profession:

> The tipoff as far as the medical profession was concerned was their adamant opposition to the transfer of the disciplinary function from the Department of Education to the Department of Health because that really scared the hell out of them, because they felt that

maybe for the first time a department of this state would begin to address itself to quality care and weed out the rotten apples. . . .

It was at a meeting of the House of Delegates of the New York State Medical Society where this greedy bunch of licensed professionals in the State of New York decided that since they couldn't get their way by reasoning or by legitimate access to the Legislature, they had to threaten the public with a doctor's strike.

I think this is the most disgraceful thing I have seen in years. These aren't wage earners working for a weekly salary, these aren't people employed by some business working on a weekly salary, these are people who are in business because we give them a license to practice. We give them the privilege to practice and earn $50,000, $60,000, $70,000, $80,000, $90,000, $100,000 a year on the lives and bodies of our citizens, and they have got a nerve to threaten this Legislature to do their dirty work for them? Well, I am not going to have any part of that, and let the word go out from me to them at least, and from others in this Legislature equally concerned, that we are not going to have any part of it, and we are not going to legislate in an atmosphere of blackmail. If doctors want to go out on strike in a criminal conspiracy to deprive patients in this state of their services, then I would like to propose we pass a bill to make that a crime or at least to make it grounds for removing their licenses. Let them go practice medicine elsewhere and not as a result of the privileges accorded to them by the State of New York and by this Legislature. Let me see from them some effort, some willingness to deal in good faith with the consuming public, their patients, in terms of their willingness to police themselves or with us in terms of elevating the standard of care.[10]

Senator Howard C. Nolan, Jr., of Albany, defended the doctors:

I honestly think we do a disservice to a . . . group of people who do an awful lot for the people in the State when we attack the doctors. I personally have a very high regard, generally speaking for most of the doctors that I have come in contact with. And, you know, it seems to me very easy to get up and take the popular stand of attacking a profession because a lot of people don't like the professions. Very interestingly enough, though, when you talk to most individuals they may criticize the doctors as a profession, but of their own doctors they always have a lot of praise for, generally speaking. No, I think the medical profession in this state has probably given us, the people of the State of New York, the best medical care not only of any state in this country but probably of any place in the world. I think it's time that we think about what the doctors do do for us.[11]

Senator Fred Isabella of Schenectady, a dentist, also disagreed with Senator Ohrenstein:

> I take exception and I disagree and I am hurt because of my leader, Minority Leader, tearing down the medical profession. For this reason, I come from a medically oriented family: one nurse, three dentists, and one physician. I'm included in that field that you speak of. My whole family is, and we serve the profession very honorably. The one, the person who tops the list on gross income are you lawyers. You lawyers. Second, the physicians. Third, the dentists. That's true, absolutely true. Now I want to say this. The reason we are in this mess today with this medical malpractice or whatever you want to call it is because of you people, maybe not this body but bodies before you who passed these laws. You are all lawyers. You messed it up and got it into this mess. . . .
>
> You lawyers, since you lost, or since you were brought into this insurance or co-insurance, whatever you want to call it, no-fault insurance, you lost one hell of a lot of business, you won't admit it. So you come and you're picking on the medical profession. You create the cases, and I'm going to show you a good example. A patient of mine who I treated dentally, my brother treated surgically, lost his legs in a train accident all right?
>
> This lawyer got a hold of the case, settled it for a million dollars, $500,000 he took for himself, this is true—$500,000 and out of the other $500,000 all expenses were paid and the guy with no legs ended up with $200,000. You didn't make any money? Who made the money? The patient?[12]

The fact that Argonaut had collected $35 million in premiums from New York State doctors and had paid out only $24,000 in claims was offered by many as proof that Argonaut had made a killing at the expense of New York State physicians and state residents. In his testimony before a congressional subcommittee, carried in the *New York Daily News,* June 17, 1975, President Baker of Argonaut said that "about 70 percent of company funds must be kept in reserve to meet expected claims. That's what we estimate we'll ultimately pay out over 20 years."

Senator Jack Bronston of Jamaica, a member of the Senate Health Committee, was among those who tried to blame the insurance industry and doctors themselves for the malpractice problem in New York State:

> The problem that was created here was created by the doctors and the Medical Society themselves. It's clear from the history of

this relationship over the past 50 years that one broker captured this business, held it, did not permit free negotiation, did not really permit the kind of policy with deductibles and geographic experience and specialty experience that was really competitive and that this contributed to a large degree to the substantial increase in premiums. Nor is it clear to me that Argonaut was not playing fast and loose itself with the doctors and patients of this state.

In the emotion of the moment, that has been lost sight of, and we have all been subjected to a kind of hysteria, which we ought now to review carefully.[13]

Senator Karen Burstein of Woodmere, Long Island, expressed the concern of some women's organizations:

I have become disturbed on the issue of informed consent and I think that my sensitivity to it is heightened because I am a woman and because there has been a great deal of evidence recently adduced that . . . women are threatened with certain paternalism by their physicians in the area for example of gynecological procedures. That some women are given drugs even though they have said they don't want to take them, not experimental drugs but drugs that do have very severe consequences for the women, and for example, the children that they then bear. I cannot see really, I mean I know what I want as a consumer of medical services. I want to know what's happening to my body. I want to know what the consequences of any particular act upon that body by a physician is going to be, and I think that I am mature enough, adult enough, to make a reasonable decision providing that both of us participated in some discussion of the medical practices that are going to proceed.[14]

The author, in his remarks during senate debate, said that the changes being proposed were not permanent solutions to the malpractice problem:

I am telling you we are going to be back here next year and the following year and the following year, fighting this problem until such time as we take the bull by the horns and change the tort system as related to medical malpractice cases.

We are going to lose doctors, not just those who are going to flee the state, but some are going to quit, go on strike, and new doctors are not going to come in to New York State. Many doctors who are at the age of retirement will give up their practice early. They are not going to leave the state but they'll quit because they can't afford to be in practice under the thrust of a malpractice crisis.

We have got to do something that is fair for patients and we have got to do something that is fair for the practitioners. . . .

> There is not enough in this legislation to make much impact on the rates of the doctors, the rates on your patients, the rates on your constituents who are going to be paying in terms of higher medical costs caused by the malpractice problem and our job is to try to solve this problem. This legislation does not do enough, we should do more.[15]

Those legislators who opposed changes in tort law were advised that some of these changes were agreed to by the State Bar Association. Doctors and lawyers created a joint Bar Association–Medical Society committee to seek a common ground of agreement on this emotional issue for both professions.

The joint committee, after many all-day meetings, agreed on most aspects of the issue. The Bar Association supported reduction in the statute of limitations and even favored abolishing the doctrine of res ipsa loquitur. The attorneys' group was opposed to admission of evidence of collateral source payments, compulsory arbitration, and a limitation of attorneys' fees. The members of the Bar Association also were against admissibility of the findings of mediation panels into evidence at a jury trial.

The state's Trial Lawyers Association, at odds with the Bar Association on many points, attempted to block passage of legislation by working through legislators who were trial lawyers or sympathetic to their views.

The head of the state's Consumer Board, who often files memorandums in support or opposition of bills, did not take a stand on the malpractice legislation. A number of groups, such as, the Committee on Patients' Rights, the Patients' Aid Society, Mothers for Educated Childbirth, the American Civil Liberties Union, and the National Organization of Women did speak out. The latter organization objected to the language of the informed consent provisions which were discussed by Senator Burstein in her remarks during the senate debate.

On April 30, the assembly passed its own malpractice bill, Assembly 6969–B. The assembly version maintained the statute of limitations at three years, and did not include any provisions for the introduction before a jury of collateral source information or the admissibility of the mediation panel's findings. In as much as a bill must be approved by both houses, this action was meaningless. For two weeks, the issue was stalemated. However, on May 15, a marathon ten-hour session in the governor's office produced the final compromise bill. This measure, Senate Bill 6449, was approved by both houses of the legislature on May 19 by overwhelming margin (56-4 in the senate and 120-27 in the assembly).

The major provisions of the legislation which was signed into law on May 21 as Chapter 109 of the Laws of 1975 are:

1. Creation of a Joint Underwriting Association for a period of six years.

2. The statute of limitations was reduced from three years to two and a half years. With respect to infants, the statute of limitations was limited to ten years after the cause of action accrues. The statute for infants was formerly to age eighteen plus three years.

3. All insurers writing malpractice coverage are required to submit detailed reports on each claim to the Superintendent of Insurance and the Commissioner of Health on a semi-annual basis.

4. The doctrine of informed consent was limited to nonemergency treatment, procedure, or surgery or diagnostic procedures which involve invasion or disruption of the integrity of the body. Lack of informed consent is defined to mean the failure of the person providing the professional treatment or diagnosis to disclose alternatives to the patient as well as reasonably foreseeable risks and benefits involved as a reasonable medical practitioner under similar circumstances would have disclosed. No action may exist unless it is established that a reasonably prudent person in the patient's position would not have undergone the treatment or diagnosis if he or she had been fully informed.

5. Evidence can be presented to a jury concerning plaintiff's payments from collateral sources such as insurance, social security, workmen's compensation, or other employee benefits.

6. If the three members of a medical malpractice panel concur on the question of liability, the panel's recommendations concerning liability may be admissible as evidence at any subsequent trial.

7. A state Board for Professional Medical Conduct was created in the Department of Health. The board consists of not fewer than eighteen physicians, two of whom shall be doctors of osteopathy and not fewer than seven lay members. The board will be responsible for the investigation and hearing of misconduct charges. Its findings, conclusions, and recommendations then go to the State Commissioner of Health, who then forwards his or her recommendation to the Board of Regents for final decision. Within sixty days

after the transfer of a case, the Board of Regents of New York State must make its final decision. The decisions of the Board of Regents are reviewable in court.

Enactment of the malpractice bill into law did not, however, bring an end to the issue for the governor and the legislature.

Many leaders of the New York State Medical Society felt that although the bill did not achieve all of the Society's objectives it was the best that they could expect considering the pressures at work inside and outside the legislature. A meeting of the House of Delegates, the Society's ultimate decision-making body, was called. Prior to that meeting, the council, which acts like an executive committee between the House of Delegates annual meetings, met in special session and gave its unanimous support to the bill approved by the legislature. The premature announcement carried widely by the news media irritated many members of the House of Delegates who thought that their role was to make such decisions.

The House of Delegates, by a vote of 143–82, opposed the new law and said that a work stoppage would be forthcoming unless the legislature enacted additional measures. Some observers said that members of the Medical Society were oversold by the society's own advertising and public relations campaign and were not willing to settle for anything less than all of the objectives they sought.

The strike threat brought on the wrath of legislators and the news media. Assemblyman Thomas J. Culhane prepared a bill which would have revoked or suspended the license of a doctor who refused to practice. The bill was co-sponsored by a large group of legislators who shared the view of its sponsor, Assemblyman Culhane, "of what I consider an almost avaricious and intransigent position by the doctors."[16]

The bill never came to a vote in the assembly or the senate.

Editorial writers who earlier had urged legislative action to assist the doctors criticized the House of Delegates statements. The Albany *Times Union* reported on April 28, 1975: "What the doctors are apparently trying to do is shift responsibility for whatever may happen to their patients to the laps of the legislators, who are burdened with a few other concerns than the incomes of the state's physicians. For let's face it—that is what is involved here, primarily, not the kind of care patients get."

On May 29, 1975, downstate physicians in Kings, Nassau, Suffolk, Rockland, Dutchess, Putnam, and Westchester counties voted to phase out medical services starting June 1, 1975, because of dissatisfaction with the new law. More than three thousand doctors on the staffs of sixteen Nassau County hospitals joined in the threat, and private physicians said they would not accept new patients in their office or schedule any elective hospital admissions.

The slowdown had an immediate effect. Brookdale Hospital in Brooklyn, for example, scheduled only twelve operations on June 2 compared with its normal forty to fifty daily surgical procedures. All elective surgery was cancelled at Mary Immaculate Hospital in Queens where the emergency room was reported to be 30 percent filled above capacity. Some downstate hospitals reported a tremendous increase in the use of their emergency facilities. These hospitals, because patients were not being admitted, were forced to lay off large numbers of employees, thereby creating an unforeseen labor problem.

It was hoped that rates for the physicians' insurance company (Medical Liability Mutual Insurance Company), approved by the State Insurance Department on May 30, would bring an end to the physicians' slowdown. The 20 percent increase was certainly a far cry from Argonaut's 196.8 percent request; however, this still did not satisfy many downstaters.

On June 4, Governor Carey and legislative leaders met with representatives of the State Medical Society and key specialty groups. Many of the rebelling doctors were members of those specialty groups hardest hit by increases.

At that conference the doctors presented a list of five items necessary for them to continue practicing in New York State: (1) definition of malpractice; (2) limit on attorneys' contingency fees; (3) an impartial medical panel to advise the jury and the court in medical malpractice cases; (4) a study commission to monitor the law and to study and recommend legislation for 1976; (5) a constitutional amendment to place a limit on jury awards, which would require approval at two legislative sessions before being put to voters in a referendum.

Senate Minority Leader Ohrenstein said the mood of the legislature was "we have done all we can." The medical profession, he added, over the years has resisted government interference. If the doctors want controls, controls can go both ways. Continuation of the job action would be counterproductive, he said.

Governor Carey announced he would appoint a Special Advisory Panel to review the entire malpractice question in New York State and monitor the effectiveness of the recently enacted legislation. The panel members would be selected by legislative leaders and the governor, with consultation with physician organizations. The panel was to report its findings and recommendations prior to the start of the 1976 session. Some recommendations could be implemented without legislative action. The governor had already conferred with the State Judicial Conference about establishing a fee schedule for attorneys in medical malpractice cases, which the Conference could do administratively, but did not.

The doctors emphasized the importance of the governor's panel to propose a legal definition of medical malpractice, and read a statement that emphasized that the doctor is not a guarantor of results.

Less than a week later, the thirty members of the doctors' crisis committee, which had spearheaded the slowdown, voted to go back to work. Norman F. Blackman, M.D., spokesman for the committee, said: "We agreed on a cooling off period but this is only a temporary suspension and we're holding the action in abeyance to see what response we get from the Governor and the Legislature." Dr. Blackman said his committee was generally pleased with those who were appointed to the governor's nine-member panel. The general feeling of the crisis committee was that suspension of the slowdown would last at least until January 1976 when the commission was to report its recommendations.[17]

The panel was chaired by Dr. William J. McGill, President of Columbia University. Other members were four legislators (including the author) two physicians, an attorney, and a hospital administrator. The vice-chairman was Herbert Tenzer, a former member of congress and senior partner of the New York City law firm of Tenzer, Greenblatt, Fallon, and Kaplan. Other members were Senator Jack E. Bronston of Jamaica, John H. Carter, M.D., of Albany, Senator John R. Dunne of Garden City, George Himler, M.D., past-president of the State Medical Society, Sister Evelyn M. Schneider, President of the Greater New York Hospital Association and Administrator of St. Vincent's Hospital in Manhattan, Assemblyman Leonard Silverman of Brooklyn, and the author.

During the fall of 1975, the governor's panel conducted hearings in Albany and New York and received testimony from a cross section of those interested in and affected by the problem. Among the questions posed to all speakers was one soliciting comment on a definition of medical malpractice. The State Department of Health in its statement said: "It would appear that there is not, or at least should not be, uncertainty about what the case law concerning malpractice is in our State. That being so, unless determinations of malpractice are to be made on some other basis than negligence, an attempt at a statutory definition is unnecessary and might well be counterproductive because of the need for judicial interpretation of whatever language was used."[18] In its report, the panel did not recommend that a definition be imposed by legislation.

A number of those testifying discussed the 1975 legislation. The New York State Bar Association said: "Some of these changes were controversial, particularly those relating to admitting findings of medical panels and evidence of collateral source payments. However, they represented constructive attempts to attack possible flaws in the legal side of the malpractice problem. These efforts should be given a chance to operate before further alterations are made in the legal system."[19]

The members of the governor's panel did not agree with the Bar Association stand and proposed further changes. Its recommendations were approved with only one dissenting vote (Senator John Dunne). The panel's recommendations are contained in Appendix F.

After the panel's report was made public, the author introduced a package of six bills, five of which sought to implement the panel's recommendations. The bills would:

1. Allow evidence of the payment of medical expenses, lost income, and other special damages in a medical malpractice action.

2. Delete the ad damnum clause which lists a special amount for damages in malpractice litigation.

3. Require itemization of verdicts in malpractice cases for pain and suffering to a maximum of $100,000.

4. Limit the recovery in malpractice cases for pain and suffering to a maximum of $100,000.

5. Create a temporary state commission on medical malpractice for a two-year period.

6. Increase, from twelve to seventeen, membership on the board of directors of the Medical Malpractice Insurance Association (the Joint Underwriting Association).

All of the proposals except increasing the membership of the Medical Malpractice Insurance Association were part of the final report of the governor's panel.

Without an apparent crisis situation as was the case in 1975, early in the 1976 session, there appeared to be little support for passage of additional malpractice legislation. However, as months passed, the plight of the hospitals drew legislative attention and then response. Hospitals were faced with increases of 200 to 500 percent in basic coverage as high as 2,000 percent in umbrella or excess coverage. The hospitals felt that their best means of survival was to be allowed to establish their own company.

Hospitals pleaded that the surplus requirement for their company be kept as low as possible since they were in an exceedingly tight fiscal bind and did not have the cash to establish a huge surplus.

Once again as was the case in the previous year, the senate was the first to act. On June 3, the senate approved two malpractice bills.

Late in June, both houses agreed on the major ingredients of a bill designed to encourage the formation of a mutual insurance company for hospitals.

The 1976 legislation, Assembly 12245, which is Chapter 966 of the Laws of 1976, provides that a total annual premium must be at least $750,000 and an initial annual surplus of $250,000 is required.

Some of its provisions are directed at making the joint underwriting association more effective and more responsive. The board of directors of the JUA is increased from twelve to fifteen. The Superintendent of Insurance now serves as a non-voting director, and he was given the authority to appoint two directors as representatives of the public. The amount of coverage hospitals can purchase from the JUA was increased to $1 million for each claimant and $10 million for all claimants in one year. Maximum coverage was previously $1 million and $3 million.

The hospital company did not apply for a license to set up business until June of 1977, when many hospitals insured by the JUA decided not to renew and instead sought coverage from the new company. Forty-seven hospitals were among the initial policyholders of the company which was to provide coverage on an occurrence basis.

Second surgical opinions, a subject of considerable controversy, were included in the 1976 bill. As part of the new law, coverage of second surgical opinions is to be included in all hospitalization policies. Initial reports received by the author on implementation of this aspect of the law shows little use being made of second surgical opinions which had been regarded by some as a means of cutting down on so-called unnecessary surgery.

Itemization of malpractice awards is another provision of the new law. Chapter 955 also eliminated the ad damnum clause in malpractice actions listing the amount of damages sought. A contingency fee schedule for plaintiffs' attorneys was established.

The schedule is as follows: 50 percent of the first $1,000; 40 percent of the next $2,000; 35 percent of the next $22,000; 25 percent of any amount over $25,000 or an amount not exceeding ⅓ of the sum recovered if the contractual agreement between client and attorney so provides.

During the 1976 legislative session, the author again expressed his concern about the effects of the continuing malpractice problem on the state's health care delivery system.

> Every day we read about practitioners who are leaving the practice of medicine in New York for a number of reasons, not just because of medical malpractice. It might be the weather, it could be taxes, it could be anything, but the straw that breaks the camel's back and the one that really gives them the impetus to look toward other jurisdictions to practice medicine in is the question of the high cost of medical malpractice in this state, and as far as New York State goes we are one of the highest rated states in the nation. There is good reason for that, because New York probably assumes most of the risks and many of the high risk cases where other states don't perform high risk sophisticated surgery. We have some of the better doctors in the State of New York and some of the best doctors are the ones that have the hardest cases, and so naturally we find that they are more vulnerable and prone to medical malpractice cases being brought.
>
> But the urgency of what we are doing here today is that it is incumbent upon this Legislature to do something to try to encourage the medical providers and the public that we can bring under control the deteriorating medical malpractice issue.[20]

During the 1977 legislative session, the author continued to press for passage of a ceiling on awards and a constitutional amendment which would permit disposition of malpractice cases by other than a jury trial. These approaches were approved in the State Senate as they were in 1976 but failed in the State Assembly.

Both houses did pass a measure designed to encourage the reporting of information concerning physician misconduct. The bill which became law on September 1, 1977, requires physicians and medical societies to report any cases of alleged misconduct to the

State Board for Professional Conduct. Those reporting such information are given immunity from any civil suit.

Fear by doctors and hospitals of litigation was believed to have reduced the number of complaints against physicians. Adoption of similar legislation in Arizona, it was claimed, resulted in a quadrupling of reported cases of alleged misconduct.

Regent Emlyn I. Griffith said the investigation and review processes in the Health Department under the 1975 law are working well, although he claimed "there is still a tendency by peer panels to protect their own." Griffith said that the Regents Committee on Professional Discipline has doubled its output in the last two years. He commented: "New York's system of professional governance is the best in the United States. What looks like a cumbersome procedure is not." Griffith suggested that emphasis be placed on making the system work, rather than on restructuring.[21]

In 1977, however, malpractice problems of ambulance services providing advanced life support services prompted introduction of a bill to permit them to buy coverage from the JUA. In several cases, ambulance services took their equipment off the road because they could not get malpractice coverage. The bill was approved by both the senate and the assembly and was signed into law by Governor Carey.

Insurance coverage for doctors and hospitals was not a problem in 1976 and 1977. Donald Fager, assistant secretary and assistant treasurer of the Medical Liability Mutual Insurance Company, the official name for the doctors' company, reported that in 1977 the firm was insuring 16,000 physicians and had $175 million in assets. Fager expressed concern over the company's inability to cancel doctors or reject them "unless they are convicted felons or drug addicts."[22]

Rates for the doctors' company were increased by 20.6 percent on July 1, 1976, and went up 15.5 percent on July 1, 1977.

When the JUA became operational in 1975, it had originally wanted a 200 percent increase for hospitals but none was approved. Rates for physicians were approved at the same level as the last Argonaut premiums. In 1976, the JUA requested a 90 percent increase for physicians and was given approval for a 20 percent increase. In 1977, the JUA again filed for a 90 percent increase for its doctor subscribers. A 15 percent increase was granted.

In an attempt to help and encourage young doctors to stay in New York, the doctors' company has offered a rate reduction to new doctors. About two hundred doctors have been given a fifty percent reduction in premiums for the first year of practice after completing training and in opening an office for the first time as a solo practitioner.

According to a study on "Hospital Malpractice Insurance in New York State," completed the winter of 1977, "the average total premium paid by hospitals for both basic and excess hospital malpractice insurance had continued to rise rapidly . . . although at a much lower rate than that associated with the sharp escalation in premiums during the prior year." Of special concern, however, was the fact "that many of the state's hospitals have reduced their malpractice insurance coverage, i.e., they are paying more for less!" The study indicated that self-insurance "is clearly a phenomenon which is here to stay. About 45 percent of the acute care beds in New York (including those of the New York City Health and Hospitals Corporation) are now entirely or partially self-insured."[23]

While claims made policies became accepted in other states the New York State Insurance Department maintained its opposition to this approach.

On February 9, 1976, the State Insurance Department conducted a hearing on "the feasibility of permitting the use of claims made medical malpractice policies in New York State." On May 7, State Insurance Superintendent Thomas A. Harnett ruled against use of claims made, a position which had been established under his predecessors and one to which he continually adhered.

In his opinion and decision, Superintendent Harnett outlined his objections to claims made. Among these were "1. the claims made form offers no long range solution to the basic medical malpractice problem. . . . 2. There would be no substantial difference in the long run between the premiums under the claims made form and the occurrence form if the premium charged each year under the occurrence form was adequate."[24]

Malpractice mediation panels, pioneered in New York State and adopted in other states, have drawn mixed reactions in New York. The Second Judicial District, covering many of the counties in the greater Metropolitan New York City area, handled 492 cases from January 1, 1975, through December 31, 1976. Of this total, 170 panel hearings were held, and 133 cases were disposed of by settlement. Ninety-five cases were disposed of at pre-panel conferences, and fifty-two cases were disposed of after panel hearings. Forty-one percent of the cases were disposed of at pre-panel conferences or after panel hearings. The total amount of the settled cases was $4,682,510.10.[25]

The Third Judicial Department, covering the Capitol District in and around Albany, had a "Success rate of better than 1 out of 3 cases" which "suggests that the panel procedure has been accepted and that attorneys prepare very thoroughly for medical malpractice mediation panel hearings in expectation of early settlement of worthwhile cases. The department had reservations about the impact of making the unanimous findings of the panel admissible in subsequent court proceedings. "The amendment has been less than enthusiastically accepted by the trial bar."[26]

The Fourth Judicial Department is strongly opposed to the panels. "On September 1, 1976, the Departmental Committee for Court Administration in the Fourth Department considered the question of medical malpractice panels. It was the unanimous recommendation that the statutory provisions creating these panels should be abolished. The reason for this was the conclusion of the attorneys and judges present that the present panels were ineffective. In particular, the judges and attorneys present thought that the panels took too much time and produced too few results. The basic problem seemed to be coordinating the schedules of busy doctors, busy attorneys, and busy judges."[27]

Arbitration which is being tried in many states was slow getting off the ground in New York. In September, 1975, the Hospital Association and the State Medical Society, in conjunction with the American Arbitration Association, announced plans to establish a voluntary arbitration program for patients, physicians, and hospitals. Before receiving medical care in a doctor's office, a patient would have the opportunity to sign a voluntary arbitration agreement referring any dispute to the American Arbitration Association. If the patient requires hospital care, he or she would be asked to sign a similar agreement with the hospital, but the patient would have the right to cancel the agreement within thirty days following discharge.

As of July 1, 1977, the Hospital Association of New York State reported that the voluntary arbitration plan had not become operational in any of its 300-member institutions. The first plan was finally started by Strong Memorial Hospital in Rochester on January 1, 1978.

Ralph S. Emerson, M.D., a past-president of the State Medical

Society, said that efforts to use arbitration had been hindered by the reluctance of the JUA to become involved with arbitration.[28]

Looking back at seven years of involvement with the malpractice issue in New York State, the author observes that a legislative body like the action of most individuals seems to forget a crisis situation once steps are taken which it feels alleviates the crisis. In fact, in the legislature, we seem to go from crisis to crisis. In trying to correct a problem, there is always the danger of over-reacting or having the solutions actually create new problems. With some issues, legislators feel that the subject is so controversial that no matter what they do, they will be criticized. Like ostriches, they hide their heads in the sand and hope the problem will go away.

Like a parent with many children, a legislator's attention is constantly shifting from one subject to another, often dealing with those who may have aroused the loudest public outcry, which does not necessarily mean they are the most critical.

The attention given the medical malpractice problem by the New York State Legislature and the general public in recent years was certainly warranted. The crisis may be over for a while, but it is a subject that will continue to come before us in New York State and elsewhere, perhaps even as dramatically as it did in 1975.

·◦[8]◦·

The Issue in Other States and Countries

ALTHOUGH THE MALPRACTICE ISSUE has had an impact on virtually every state in this country, some, such as California and Indiana, have received much of the attention from the nation's news media. California gained prominence because of work slowdowns by doctors, while Indiana's new malpractice law was hailed as landmark legislation by members of the country's medical profession.

California had two strikes within a year. The first began in May, 1975, when anesthesiologists in San Francisco protested a proposed increase of 385 percent in insurance premiums by Argonaut. They were joined by some surgeons in a slowdown which continued for nearly a month and spread to six counties in the Bay Area.

The second protest in Southern California started on January 1, 1976, in response to a request by Travellers to hike their premiums by 487 percent.

The Southern California doctors urged Governor Edmund G. Brown, Jr., to call the legislature into special session to take further action on the malpractice issue.

Members of a group known as the Ad Hoc Committee of Concerned Physicians from the San Fernando Valley–Los Angeles area met with Governor Brown along with other representatives of the medical profession, including the president of the California Medical Association. The doctors demanded further tightening of tort reforms, including a one-year statute of limitations and immediate relief from skyrocketing malpractice premiums.

This committee advocated governmental assistance in the form of a state fund to subsidize any awards or settlements over $50,000 which would limit the physician's liability to $50,000. Financing of the fund, according to committee members, would be obtained either through a tax on health insurance premiums or a $200 assessment for each physician as part of the state medical licensing fee. Over a three-year period, the committee maintained that the fund could reduce premiums by one third.[1]

Governor Brown said: "Statistics showed that in recent months about 14 per cent of those bringing malpractice suits in California received favorable verdicts from juries. If governmental funds were made available to ease the burden on doctors and insurance companies, the number of suits would rise and the judgments might reach 50 percent."[2]

In the California legislature, proposed governmental subsidies, according to Assemblyman Barry Keene, chairman of the Assembly Health Committee, drew opposition from both liberals and conservatives. Keene said: "Liberals feel 'why should we subsidize the most affluent profession?' Conservatives are opposed because they view it as another step toward subsidized socialized medicine."[3]

When Brown failed to call a special session or take other action, the second California strike began. An estimated 23,000 physicians participated in a thirty-five-day job action. The only major concession won by the strikers was a rollback by the State Insurance Commissioner of the premium increase to 327 percent.

Joseph T. Boyle, M.D., a Los Angeles internist who left his practice for six months in 1975 to lobby for malpractice legislation on behalf of the California Medical Association, said: "The reason that doctors in the South went on strike was because they were told that the reason you got anything at all from the Legislature in 1975 was because doctors in the North went on strike."[4] Boyle and others admit that the early 1976 job action ended as increased criticism began to come from the news media.

Assemblyman Keene downplayed the strikes and slowdowns and instead emphasized the legislative accomplishments in attempting to solve the malpractice issue. Keene, speaking at a national conference of state legislators in October 1975, stated:

> Nineteen seventy-five was the year that California passed a major comprehensive medical malpractice bill. As an occasion of historic note, it is marked far more by what did not happen than what did. Twenty-five thousand physicians did not walk out. The acute care hospitals throughout the State did not close down. Nurses and other associated health care personnel are not in the unemployment lines. Physicians and the bill paying public are not so dismayed with

government's failure to respond that they are not making every reasonable and prudent effort to deal with a one-time premium cost adjustment in the neighborhood of 300 to 500 percent.

We almost did not pass the measure. So the observations that
I make must be greatly tempered by that fact. Nor is AB 1 (the designation for the legislation) of our Second Extraordinary Session, therefore affectionately referred to by the trial lawyers as AB 1 Double
Cross, universally acclaimed. Nor should it be. It is not perfect because we do not have the empirical data to create a perfect response. And it is not perfect in the eyes of one group that demands
immediate total relief, or in the eyes of another with a clear self-
serving interest and one-dimensional perspective.[5]

Keene noted that this legislation is a three-part measure consisting of a new procedure on discipline, tort reform and insurance
provisions. The Assembly Health Committee Chairman said that
there is no longer a lifetime doctor's license in California. The bill
provides a four to six year continuing education requirement with
each applicant having to prove competence at the end of each such
period as a condition of continued licensure.

The board supervising the disciplining process has been
equipped with its own investigators, and consumer representation
has been increased from one to seven members. The governing body
has the power to revoke, suspend, restrict, or limit the scope of a
doctor's practice.

Keene continued that reports of findings, action taken, settlements, judgments, and restrictions upon a doctor must be submitted
to a central registry "where individual profile reviews to ascertain
aberrant practice are undertaken." District peer review, he maintained, has also been strengthened.

The California bill, according to Keene, incorporates to some
degree virtually every proposed tort reform where an identifiable
cost saving could be identified. There is a ninety-day notice requirement before a malpractice suit can be filed. An elaborate three-year
statute of limitations was enacted, except in cases of fraud or those
involving minors.

A sliding scale of attorneys' fees for malpractice cases was
established by the new California law. Keene said that the provisions also included restructured awards to be paid on a periodic
basis "to prevent windfalls to non-dependent heirs." The prohibition
against introduction of information on collateral source was eliminated, and permissive but binding arbitration was approved. A ceil-

ing of $250,000 has been set on awards "on subjective or non-economic losses."[6]

The California State Insurance Commissioner is mandated to respond to complaints of excessive rates for malpractice insurance by conducting a public hearing. Representatives of physician and consumer groups have the right to cross-examine speakers at the hearings.

The Insurance Commissioner has the power to roll back rates which he judges to be excessive and, if private companies pull out, to create a nonprofit joint underwriting association. Assemblyman Keene said that independent actuaries would set rates for the JUA which is required to offer a two-year claims made insurance policy on an emergency basis, with a guaranteed occurrence rider to be picked up at the end of that time.

While New York State doctors formed one physician-owned company (see Chapter 7), California has several doctors' companies. This diversity within the state of California or the disposition to have a regional approach rather than one statewide plan is one which seems prevalent not only in the field of medicine but in many other areas of activity within California.

The Norcal Mutual Insurance Company was set up for physicians in Northern California. Also created were the Southern California Physicians Insurance Exchange and the Medical Insurance Exchange (Bay Area counties), and the Doctors' Company was offering coverage to doctors throughout the State.

Clarence Atwood, chief actuary for the California Insurance Department, differs from many observers on the future of doctors companies. Atwood sees the companies as a permanent solution to the problem of providing malpractice insurance for doctors.[7]

The California Medical Association has helped fund a $750,000 study which is a review of 20,000 patient charts at hospitals. The study will establish the protocol for identifying occurrences. The California Medical Association is interested in identifying the differences in cost between a fault and a no-fault system and in determining if we as a society can support a no-fault system. The California Hospital Association believes that this will give it a means to establish an early warning system.[8]

In 1976, the California legislature authorized the establishment of a tort reform commission, consisting of ten members. Hearings are to be held in 1978 and the commission is to report by March

1979. Another group, the California Citizens' Commission on Tort Reform issued its report in September 1977 (see Appendix G).

Like California, Florida in 1975 also seemed headed for a large-scale withdrawal of medical services in two populous areas on its famed Gold Coast (Dade and Broward Counties). Members of the Dade County Medical Association, based in Miami, voted to withhold all but emergency services. This action never materialized, but some doctors in adjoining Broward County, which includes the Fort Lauderdale area, did participate in a two-week job action, reducing surgery by 85 percent.[9]

Proposed premium increases by Argonaut Insurance Company in March 1975 precipitated the Florida crisis. Argonaut succeeded Employers Insurance of Wausau as the carrier for the Florida State Medical Association in 1973. Miami Attorney Steven R. Berger said: "The new rates announced by the company were more than double the rates in January (1975) which had already nearly doubled from the prior year." Berger claimed that "a neurosurgeon with a perfect claims report had already gone from $5,771 to $10,728 and was now raised to $20,000 with a mid-year increase to around $33,000 expected."[10] After extensive court proceedings, on May 19, 1975, Argonaut's Florida rates were ruled invalid in United States District Court. By that time, the Florida legislature had unanimously approved its response to the crisis which included the establishment of a Temporary Joint Underwriting Association.

Florida doctors were incensed when the TJUA rates approved by the State Insurance Commissioner on June 24, 1975, were higher than those sought by Argonaut. Berger said: "A Dade County cardiac surgeon was charged $3,543 per year prior to January 1, 1975. This rose to $6,583, and Argonaut's April proposal would have been $12,835. Under TJUA the rate for the policy is now $15,154."[11] According to Berger, the next step for Florida hospitals and physicians is self-insurance which is permitted under the law.

In the state of Indiana, State Senator Adam Benjamin, a sponsor of that state's well-publicized bill, said "most of us did not know the impact of medical malpractice until the 1975 session." Benjamin pointed out that Indiana Governor Otis R. Bowen, a physician, had played a major role in the successful enactment of the legislation. Senator Benjamin said that the bill had widespread support including that of the AFL-CIO but that several legislators who voted for it claimed it was "an insurance rip-off."[12]

Governor Bowen claimed that Indiana's malpractice crisis "cut down the flow of new physicians into Hoosier practice, and forced the early retirement or major cutback of practice by a number of Hoosier doctors already in practice." Governor Bowen highlighted the fact that all interested parties to the malpractice issue in his state had to give in on some points. "In the true spirit of compromise, the bill that emerged was viewed to be fair to all concerned, acceptable to all concerned but not wholly to the liking of any single party."[13]

Gavin Lodge, a staff attorney in the Indiana legislature, said the malpractice crisis in that state emerged after six anesthesiologists in a large hospital were notified that their malpractice coverage would not be renewed. According to Lodge, the basic problem in Indiana was not excessive rates but the fear that malpractice insurance would become unavailable.[14]

The Indiana law has a recovery limit of $500,000 applied to hospitals, clinical psychologists, dentists, and many other types of health providers. To be covered by the act, each health provider must file proof of insurance up to $100,000. Awards over $100,000 under provisions of the law are to be paid out of a Patient's Compensation Fund, which is financed through a surcharge on the malpractice premiums of health care providers. The statute of limitations in Indiana has been reduced to two years for malpractice claims. Claims for minors under the age of six, however, may be filed up to a child's eighth birthday.

The insurance provisions of the Indiana law provided for a "risk manager," a post that after bidding was awarded to the Medical Protective Company of Fort Wayne, Indiana. The risk manager must deal with the problems of availability of insurance in high-risk cases. A health provider who is denied insurance by two carriers may apply for coverage through the risk manager, who is compensated for services rendered on a percentage of premiums basis.

The Indiana law created a Medical Review Panel consisting of three physicians and one non-voting attorney. The panel must review all malpractice claims prior to the initiation of any legal action.

The plaintiff and the defendant each select one physician to sit on the panel. The physicians chosen by the plaintiff and the defendant then pick the third panel member. In some cases, health care providers other than physicians may serve on the panel. The panel's findings may be admissable as evidence at a jury trial and panel members may be called as witnesses.

A 15 percent limit for attorneys' fees has been imposed for any awards allocated from the Patient's Compensation Fund, and the ad damnum clause (a specific amount in damages) has been eliminated. The appropriate licensing agency in the state must receive information on all claims settled or adjudicated to final judgment.

Lodge pointed out that the Indiana law does not make provisions for multiple defendants. He said that if there were five defendants, there is a possibility that the plaintiff could recover five $100,000 awards and that such cases would not be paid by the Patient's Compensation Fund. If one attorney handled all of the claims in the case, the contingency fee limit on awards could be circumvented.

Lodge said that the Indiana legislature should be applauded for acting with dispatch in dealing with a very complex issue under very trying and difficult circumstances. He contended that actions were based on sketchy, if not suspect information. Further, he said, quick action to some extent was forced on public officials by the glaring headlines found daily on the front pages of the newspapers and in radio and television editorials and news programs, which in his mind, overdramatized a problem into a crisis.

He recommended that the situation in Indiana and in other states requires stricter regulation of insurance rates by regulatory agencies, especially in the area of insurance company reserves. Some observers point to the fact that the highest judgment ever awarded in a malpractice suit in Indiana is $212,000, and that there has never been an award for punitive damages. These factors lead some to "believe that talk of crisis was verbal overkill."[15]

In the spring of 1977, Governor Bowen reported that Indiana had thirty-three cases "filed for medical review panel appointment, with no settlements exceeding the $100,000 insurance coverage mandatorily required."[16] There have been no major increase in malpractice insurance rates since 1975.[17]

Syndicated newspaper columnist Sylvia Porter was high in her praise for the new Michigan law which she said "may become the model for national legislation to end the spiral in medical malpractice insurance costs and thereby to help curb medical costs for all of us." Columnist Porter cited the binding contractual arbitration aspects of the Michigan law which she described as "an arrangement under which the patient signs an arbitration agreement." She said the binding arbitration program "could produce insurance and legal savings of 20 to 30 per cent, to be passed on to patients." Instead of standard awards, an arbitrator might decide that the plaintiff be given surgery, free of charge, to correct a condition judged to have been aggravated by the defendant's action. Other alternatives for the arbitrator would be the awarding of convalescent care or the establishment of a trust fund "to continue for the life of the patient and then revert to the insurer."[18]

Pennsylvania also enacted a statewide arbitration system, administered by the Office of Medical Malpractice Arbitration. The office set up a panel to handle each claim. Parties in the arbitration action retain the right to file an appeal and to receive a jury trial, however, the appealant can be liable for the cost of the trial.

The insurance provisions of the Pennsylvania statute require every health care provider to insure his liability by purchasing professional liability insurance in the amount of $100,000 per occurrence and $300,000 per annual aggregate. The state's new Medical Professional Liability Catastrophe Loss Fund "shall pay all awards in excess of $100,000 per annual aggregate."[19]

The first administrator of the Office of Medical Malpractice Arbitration, was Paul F. Abrams, a former aide to Senator Edward M. Kennedy. He said that claims will be handled more expeditiously and that limits on insurance coverage will also save money.[20]

Table 11 summarizes the malpractice legislation approved in 1975 and 1976. In summary, some of the changes are as follows: Ad damnum clauses (25 states); statute of limitations (35 states); Itemized verdicts (3 states); Locality rules (15 states); expert witnesses (9 states); res ipsa loquitur (7 states); informed consent (20 states); notice of intent to sue (14 states); attorney fee regulations (19 states); joint underwriting associations (31 states); captive companies (11 states); state fund (5 states); insurance pools (4 states); assigned risk (4 states); mandatory insurance for health care providers (14 states); incident or claim reporting (31 states); arbitration (10 states); pretrial screening panels (17 states).[21]

As expected, the malpractice legislation adopted in many states faced quick court challenges. Governor Otis R. Bowen of Indiana said: "These days people tend to challenge almost anything. I have no quarrel with this. If there is a cloud over any portion of the (Indiana) law, it is just as well that it be challenged so that what is done in the future will be under the protection of the courts."[22]

As of this writing court challenges have been filed in fifteen states.

The $500,000 ceiling on awards in Illinois, for example, was ruled as unconstitutional by that state's Supreme Court. The highest courts in Idaho and Nebraska ruled that limitations on awards were unconstitutional.

A lower court in Ohio threw out limits of $200,000 for noneconomic damages in medical malpractice cases.

While the Illinois Supreme Court struck down the mandatory pre-trial screening panels, the panels were upheld in New York, Nebraska, and Florida.

A lower court in Tennessee "ruled that the mandatory submission of medical malpractice claims to a review board prior to court action violates Tennessee's constitutional guarantee of free and open access to its courts without delay." Illinois, North Carolina and Kentucky courts declared insurance provisions in those states' medical malpractice legislation are unconstitutional. Oregon's Supreme Court refused to consider the constitutionality of the Oregon Medical Malpractice Act. Florida's entire medical malpractice statute was declared unconstitutional "since the statute violated a section of the Florida Constitution which prohibits enactment of statutes embracing more than one subject.[23] A new law was adopted in 1977.

In Michigan, the makeup of the arbitration panels was challenged. Sheldon Miller, a Detroit attorney, has questioned the role of a doctor on a panel which he said puts the doctor into a conflict of interest situation since his own malpractice insurance premium might be affected by his decision as a panelist. Miller commented: "His own premium will rise or fall because of his action." Miller maintained that in our court system "we strive to have a jury or a judge who have no preconceived notions or ideas about a case."[24]

Dr. Joseph Boyle of the California Medical Association noted that more laws are created by the courts these days than by the legislature.[25] This is a fact of life that holds true not only with respect to medical malpractice but to virtually all issues considered by state legislatures, the United States Senate, and the House of Representatives.

There is a strong negative feeling among some legislators and some members of the general public that instead of being a check on the legislative and executive branches as was the design of our founding fathers that our courts have become the ultimate decision-making body in the country.

Another point of view is expressed by Professor William J.

Table 11

SUMMARY OF STATE MEDICAL MALPRACTICE LEGISLATION

	Alabama	Alaska	Arizona	Arkansas	California	Colorado	Connecticut	Delaware	Florida	Georgia	Hawaii	Idaho	Illinois	Indiana	Iowa	Kansas	Kentucky	Louisiana	Maine	Maryland	Massachusetts	Michigan	Minnesota	Mississippi	Missouri
Ad Damnum	X	X	X		X				X	X	X	X	X	X	X	X	X	X	X		X	X			
Advance Payment	X	X					X	X		X			X			X			X	X	X				
Attorney Fee			X		X				X			X	X			X	X	X			X		X		
Awarding Costs														X											
Collateral Source			X		X				X	X			X	X		X	X				X				
Informed Consent									X					X											
Itemized Verdict	X		X		X	X			X	X	X	X	X	X	X	X		X		X		X	X	X	X
Statute of Limitations			X		X				X				X			X				X	X				
Special Statute For Minors					X								X			X				X					
Limitation On Recovery	X	X	X	X					X	X			X			X				X					
Standard Of Care									X	X				X		X				X			X		
Expert Witness			X	X					X	X			X							X					
Burden of Proof					X																				
Notice Of Intent To Sue	X	X			X				X	X									X		X				
Periodic Payment	X	X			X				X	X						X			X	X					
Statute Of Frauds	X	X	X		X	X		X	X			X	X	X		X		X		X	X			X	X
JUA			X						X							X				X					
Captive Company (Legislation)											X					X			X	X		X	X		
Assigned Risk Pools		X					X		X		X	X		X		X	X								
Mandatory Insurance	X	X	X			X	X		X			X	X	X	X		X	X	X		X		X	X	
Mandatory Claim Reporting									X																
Channeling								X				X		X			X		X	X	X				
Excess Recovery Fund	X	X			X											X				X			X		
Arbitration		X	X	X					X	X		X	X		X			X		X	X	X			
Pre-Trial Screening		X	X	X					X	X		X	X			X		X		X	X				

	Montana	Nebraska	Nevada	New Hampshire	New Jersey	New Mexico	New York	North Carolina	North Dakota	Ohio	Oklahoma	Oregon	Pennsylvania	Rhode Island	South Carolina	South Dakota	Tennessee	Texas	Utah	Vermont	Virginia	Washington	West Virginia	Wisconsin	Wyoming
Ad Damnum	X			X	X	X		X				X			X		X			X			X	X	X
Advance Payment	X	X		X									X				X				X	X	X		
Attorney Fee	X		X	X				X			X	X	X				X				X		X		
Awarding Costs	X										X	X													
Collateral Source	X	X		X				X			X		X				X				X				
Informed Consent	X	X		X	X			X			X	X					X				X				
Itemized Verdict				X																					
Statute of Limitations	X	X		X	X	X	X	X	X		X			X	X	X	X			X					X
Special Statute For Minors				X	X	X							X				X	X							X
Limitation On Recovery	X			X				X				X		X						X			X		
Standard Of Care	X	X			X			X				X					X				X				
Expert Witness		X						X	X								X								
Burden Of Proof	X	X			X			X				X					X	X			X				
Notice Of Intent To Sue				X													X	X							
Periodic Payment	X				X			X				X					X	X							
Statute Of Frauds	X	X	X		X	X		X				X	X	X	X		X	X		X			X		
JUA						X			X							X	X								
Captive Company (Legislation)	X		X					X		X			X							X			X		
Assigned Risk Pools	X				X	X				X	X						X	X					X		
Mandatory Insurance	X			X	X	X		X	X		X	X	X		X	X	X		X			X	X		X
Mandatory Claim Reporting								X																	
Channeling	X			X	X	X			X	X		X			X		X						X		
Excess Recovery Fund						X						X			X				X	X					
Arbitration	X	X		X	X						X		X			X						X			X

Source: State Health Legislation Report, Legislative Department, Public Affairs Division, American Medical Association, Chicago, Illinois, Volume 5, Number 1, May 1977.

Curran of Harvard. Curran, noting that many of the legislative approaches to medical malpractice have been challenged in the courts, said:

> A very large part of the reform enacted in 1975 is subject to these challenges. The basic point is that the legislation selects only one group for special treatment (class legislation) without clear justification for the discrimination. Why should recoveries against physicians be restricted when unlimited amounts can be recovered from all others tortfeasors? Why should contingent percentage fees be restricted in malpractice cases, but not in other personal injury areas and other areas of law practice? Percentage recoveries of all sort are common in many other enterprises, not merely in the legal system. For more fundamental reform, the medical community is going to need to recruit allies from other areas. Further research may be needed, either to justify the special discriminatory legislation in malpractice, or to support the enactment of the changes in other fields.[26]

In some jurisdictions, the court challenges have served to minimize the impact of legislation on malpractice premiums. Many insurance carriers and insurance commissioners are reluctant to lower premiums "until the constitutional issues raised by the new legislation are resolved."[27]

Discussion of rising malpractice rates in most parts of the United States often brings out the fact that malpractice rates elsewhere in the world are much lower. Because of the vast differences in the health care delivery and legal systems, accurate conclusions may not be drawn by comparing the United States and other countries. For the most part, the increase in malpractice premiums, suits, and awards has not affected other nations.

A national slowdown by doctors in Great Britain which started in the late fall of 1975 had serious implications for that country's National Health Service and could have some effects related to the malpractice issue. On December 10, 1975, the father of a five-month-old girl blamed her death on the slowdown. The man said the child died after she was refused admission to two hospitals.

According to an Associated Press dispatch from London, "about half of the country's 19,000 junior hospital doctors are working 9 A.M. to 5 P.M. only in a nationwide pay dispute with the labor government and many hospital emergency wards now close at 5 P.M."[28]

Whether the girl's death and any other subsequent events will result in legal action remains to be seen. The liability of practitioners and health care facilities during a slowdown is a question that has greatly concerned many persons inside and outside of the health care delivery system in the United States.

On the subject of malpractice rates in Great Britain, *Medical World News* reported that malpractice coverage generally costs $58.25 a year. The coverage includes "unlimited malpractice insurance without regard to speciality, the number of past claims, or the size of past settlements, a sophisticated legal and ethical counseling service and a team of expert attorneys."[29]

George A. Friedman, M.D., outlined the system in the United Kingdom in testimony to two New York State legislative committees:

> There are three medical defense organizations in the United Kingdom. The Medical Defense Union has 65,000 members—the Medical Protection Society has 56,000 doctors and dentists working in the United Kingdom, New Zealand, Australia, South Africa, the Caribbean, Canada, and many other countries. The third organization is the Medical and Dental Defense Union of Scotland. . . .
>
> The average amount paid out in malpractice claims is $5,200.
>
> They [defense societies] believe that the protection of the doctor is better safeguarded by a defense organization than by an insurance company. These are nonprofit-making organizations. Every claim is judged on its merits and it is only very rarely that a claim is settled because it would be cheaper to settle out of court rather than to resist it and incur high legal costs. All protection organizations are run by a council selected from the membership and consists of doctors of a very wide range of expertise. They employ a professional secretariat and the medical protection society has six doctors and two dentists who are full time and advise members and handle claims in conjunction with the societies' lawyers.
>
> The defense societies say that they differ from insurance companies in that the interest of the individual practitioners is paramount. There have been cases that they wanted to litigate as test cases but the members' interest required settlement. Equally, they litigate many cases on points of principle which would not be litigated by commercial insurance companies. They point out there is no move to attempt to exclude doctors from the normal operating laws of negligence. Since 1950 a would-be plaintiff has but to convince a legal aid committee that he has a prima facie case and he will then be assessed as to what financial contribution, if any, he should make. All doctors employed in the national health service hospitals in the United Kingdom and in the Republic of Ireland are required to be members of a protective or defense society. Thus, these defense societies protect physicians if through what the law calls negligence and

a patient suffers harm, they make money available for compensation to the patient.

The Canadian Medical Protective Association covers Canada. Of the 28,000 practicing physicians there, 23,000 belong to defense unions and membership costs $50 a year. The largest award in Canada has been for $100,000, but most awards have been for less than $45,000. The Canadian Association wrote, "our problems here in Canada are obviously different than yours in the United States because of the difference in the legal system of the two countries."[30]

In the year 1973, "there were only 163 writs served on Canadian doctors (62 in 1969) and only 44 of these went to court. Most actions are either discontinued by the plaintiff or dismissed by the courts." In 1973, the Canadian Medical Protective Association paid out only $325,087 in damages against the doctors it insures, which comprise 80 percent of the physicians in Canada. Malpractice premiums were increased from $50 to $100 in 1975.[31]

In his testimony Dr. Friedman told the New York State legislative committees on October 4, 1974, of correspondence that he had with sixty medical societies around the globe. Some responses to Dr. Friedman's inquiries were as follows:

Pakistan Medical Association—"People actually shy away from courts because there is a shortage of doctors and the social prestige of the doctor is very high."

Indian Medical Association—"The uneducated in India still regard illness as an act of God and they rarely blame a doctor for an unfavorable outcome. The cost of coverage is $5.05 for $4,500 insurance and $18 a year for $145,000."

Israel—"Most of the physicians are employees of the state and when there are malpractice claims they are submitted to the institutions where the physicians are employed."

Norway—"Less than five claims a year and the cost of insurance is $10 a year for coverage of $42,000 to $85,000. The highest claim ever paid in that country is $7,000."

Denmark—"The fairly quiet picture of the whole matter in this country is a consequence of our legal system since these matters are not settled by a jury but by a court manned by judges."

Finland—"Insurance costs between $11 and $33 and the average settlement has been $1,500."

Holland—"Malpractice is no problem at all since lawyers and courts are reluctant to call doctors to court or to condemn them in any way."

Despite the high cost of health care, and all problems inherent to the malpractice issue in the United States, it is doubtful if many legislators or other Americans would choose to have complex medical procedures performed in other countries.

The Calm Before Another Crisis

T HE GENERAL PUBLIC and most legislators believed that the medical malpractice issue was resolved when corrective legislation described in Chapters 7 and 8 provided for the continuation of malpractice insurance coverage for doctors and hospitals. On the surface everything seemed to be under control.

By 1977, doctors in more than a dozen states had banded together to form their own insurance companies which in some circles became known as "bedpan mutuals." Hospitals quickly followed suit, and within the period of a year twenty hospital insurance companies were conceived and established.

Hospitals across the country were helped considerably in late winter of 1977 when the Bureau of Health Insurance for HEW issued guidelines on reimbursement for malpractice insurance premiums. The HEW guidelines stated:

> The Medicare program reimbursement requirements have now been modified to be compatible with a number of alternatives which providers may find to be economically preferable to obtaining commercial malpractice and comprehensive general patient liability insurance coverage. Thus, the program will allow reimbursement for its share of the reasonable cost a provider incurs in protecting itself against malpractice and comprehensive general patient liability losses where the provider chooses a form of liability protection other than traditional commercial insurance. Depending on the manner in which the provider seeks to protect itself against malpractice losses, the program will reimburse the provider for the appropriate share of the net reasonable costs incurred for premiums on a commercial insurance policy, premium payments to a limited purpose insurance company, payments set aside for a self-insurance plan, or actual claims paid arising out of reasonable deductible provisions.[1]

125

These and other developments served to create the impression that the crisis, if one ever existed, was over. The *Wall Street Journal* was one of many publications taking this optimistic viewpoint. An April 19, 1977, front-page story reported that "the medical-malpractice-insurance malaise, which not long ago seemed incurable, is getting better."

St. Paul Fire and Marine Insurance Company, one of the few private carriers to remain in the field through its claims-made policy reduced its 1977 doctors' medical malpractice insurance rates in seventeen states. According to the company, these states accounted for 80 percent of the physicians and surgeons it insures. The St. Paul also expected to reduce hospital malpractice insurance rates in a number of states. Waverly G. Smith, president of St. Paul, said: "We're convinced we made the right decision in not abandoning medical malpractice insurance. We're cautiously optimistic about our ability to continue profitable operations. . . . We look to the future with renewed confidence."[2]

The availability of insurance coverage and a decline in malpractice suits and awards were regarded as proof that calm had returned to the malpractice front. Some cited increased awareness of jurors as the most significant reason for the drop in awards.

Bernard Hirsch, counsel for the American Medical Association, quipped: "People on juries are reading the newspapers." James Ludlam, a member of HEW's Medical Malpractice Commission and the American Bar Association's Commission on Medical Professional Liability, said: "Publicity has created a different public attitude."[3]

Young and old heard and read much about malpractice in the 1970s as illustrated by the following anecdote: A twelve-year-old boy accompanied his mother to the hospital emergency room after she sprained her ankle. The youngster was fascinated by the surroundings in the hospital. His father later asked the boy if he would want to become a doctor. "No," exclaimed the youth, "I don't want to be sued for medical malpractice!"

Malcolm Todd, M.D., a past-president of the American Medical Association, pointed to the use of counter-suits as another reason for a decline in medical malpractice suits.[4] Among the more publicized counter-suits was that brought by Leonard Berlin, a Chicago radiologist who had been sued for $250,000. Dr. Berlin sued the woman patient, her attorney husband, and the two attorneys who represented her for "maliciously bringing suit against him without reasonable basis and for negligence by the attorneys in not adequately investigating the merits of the case before filing the law suit." Berlin was awarded $8,000, and the court "found the attorneys and their client to be guilty of 'willful and wanton behavior' in failing to investigate the factors before filing a lawsuit against Dr. Berlin."[5]

Also encouraging were signs of improvement in disciplining of doctors which formerly had been a very slow and seldom used process. According to James H. Sammons, M.D., executive vice-president of the American Medical Association, an AMA survey in thirty-five states showed that "the number of disciplinary actions initiated against physicians by state medical licensure boards has increased from 277 in 1971 to 936 in 1976. Revocations of physicians licenses jumped from 74 in 1974 to over 139 in 1976."[6] In New York decisions rendered by the Board of Regents on medical discipline cases increased more than 50 percent and the mean time from the final peer hearing to disposition by the Board of Regents was reduced by 40 percent.[7]

The rare event of a doctor suing two colleagues on Long Island was seen by others as a sign of changing times. Two doctors on Long Island faced a $2.75 million suit in connection with the birth eight years earlier of the brain-damaged daughter of a gynecologist.[8]

Doctors and hospitals were giving increased attention to improving communications with patients. Openness and frankness can ease even the most trying of situations such as the case of a surgeon who operated on the wrong eye for cataracts. The doctor quickly reported the incident to the insurance company and was told to discuss it immediately with the patient. The second surgery was done a few days later and the case was settled for a few thousand dollars.[9]

The increasing use of patient advocates or patient ombudsmen helped improve communications. The Massachusetts General Hospital was acknowledged as a leader in this field. Its patient care representatives program was inaugurated in 1973. Isabella Tighe, head of the office, who had been a premed student and has a master's degree in business administration, admitted that it took two years for her to get the confidence of people inside the hospital. In 1976 the office had 1500 contacts or complaints. Patient grievance mechanisms are expected to increase following a June 1976 mandate by the Federal Government that as part of Medicare's chronic renal (kidney) disease program that all such medical facilities providing such care must have a patients' bill of rights and a patients' grievance mechanism.[10]

Ms. Tighe feels that it is a necessity for a hospital to have someone in the hospital who is not part of the treatment team to handle complaints. Since the person is not part of the treatment team, the patient's fear of registering a complaint is lessened. She emphasized, however, that the consumer (the patient) has a vital responsibility in this process—to ask the right question. Ms. Tighe commented: "A patient will say I didn't understand him but the patient failed to ask follow-up questions."[11]

The total health care delivery system, like government bureaucracy, has become so big that the patient, like the average citizen and taxpayer, often does not think that he or she can turn to anyone who will listen to complaints and propose ways to correct a problem or complaint.

In recent years, many legislative offices have devoted more and more time to serving as an ombudsman for constituents who do not know where else to turn whether it be medical malpractice or any other issue.

Among other non-legislative offshoots of the medical malpractice crisis of 1975 was the establishment by the American Bar Association of its Commission on Medical Professional Liability. Funded at $200,000 a year, the commission was originally scheduled to complete its work within two years, but was extended for a third year. Funding was 37 percent by the Bar Association and a similar amount from HEW with some small grants making up the difference.

Lyman M. Tondell of New York City, a past-president of the New York State Bar Association, was appointed chairman of the commission. Tondell explained that the Bar Association was aware of the inter-professional back-biting on medical malpractice and in partial response authorized the establishment of the fifteen-member body.[12]

The Bar Association Commission, according to James Ludlam, was in a more advantageous position than its HEW predecessor. "We now have some information whereas in the HEW report we dealt strictly from ignorance." He maintained that the Bar Association Commission was very sophisticated and its members were able to debate issues. He believed that the quality of the debate and the end product were much better, conceding, however, that the second time around, "everything is easier."[13] (see Appendix H)

Ludlam stated that consumerism clouded deliberations of the HEW Commission and the ability to get down to the hard issues. This statement may rankle consumer advocates but is understood by some legislators, and others who do not accept as gospel every utterance of consumer advocates. Many of their well-intentioned ideas which they offer as unnegotiable demands add rather than reduce the costs of products and services. They should have a voice and a role in decision-making but certainly not the only voice. I am reminded of a comment heard during the campus uprisings of the 1960s—"it is far from clear that those making the most noise make the most sense."

From talking with legislators across the country who were involved in key deliberations about medical malpractice in their states it is evident that consumer advocates for the most part did not seek or play important roles during the malpractice crisis.

Trial lawyers in most instances sought to portray themselves as the spokesmen for patients and consumers.

Improved monitoring of patient records in hospitals should provide better early warning systems as to new procedures which might be troublesome and practitioners who might be in need of upgrading or should be restricted in what they can and cannot do.

John S. Boyden, Jr., M.D., president of the American College of Legal Medicine, pointed out the benefits of such monitoring. "If hospitals knew what were their current injury problems, they could plan continuing education which could be meaningful and appropriate, make changes in procedures which might limit the risk of injury and make the injury the subject of future research."[14]

All of the aforementioned presents a rosy picture about medical malpractice which the author believes is shallow and distorted. Legislation and other approaches have been a finger in the dike or band aid procedure when major surgery is required. In seeking to dispel the notion that the malpractice issue has been permanently resolved, we must consider several factors and problems.

Despite the suspected decline in claims the cost of settling cases goes up 15 percent a year.[15]

The halt in the rise of malpractice claims, the author fears, is merely temporary. Some experts, like Bernzweig, think that we have just seen the tip of the iceberg. Bernzweig noted that the HEW Commission studies had shown that 30 percent of potential malpractice claims reported by doctors and hospitals to their own insurance carriers "never materialized as claims by patients. What this tells me and should tell you, is that we are not looking at a malpractice claims crisis yet. That is a few years ahead of us, when the public begins filing claims at greater and greater rates, catching up with what I consider is a claims filing lag."[16]

Self-insurance, an avenue being explored and utilized by some hospitals, was a source of growing concern. Arthur J. Mannix, Jr., president of the doctors' company in New York, expressed doubts about the hospitals' self-insurance plans continuing without regulation. Mannix said: "In the absence of departmental regulation it is frighteningly apparent that some hospitals have not and will not establish a reserve fund sufficient to pay anticipated losses. . . . These practices can only lead to dire consequences when the institutions in question are unable to respond in damages to an injured party who is legitimately entitled to compensation." Mannix urged the State require all hospitals involved in self-insurance for medical malpractice must have such a plan approved by the State Insurance Department.[17]

Hospital companies, doctors' companies, and joint underwriting associations, for example, have experienced difficulty in excess coverage (sometimes called umbrella or disaster coverage) and reinsurance.

The Harvard University and its affiliated teaching institutions paid $1.7 million for $45 million of excess coverage for claims $5 million and above in its first year of operation. For the second year, excess coverage cost $2.3 million for coverage of $40 million for claims above $10 million. Daniel P. Creasey, head of the company, said: "As you can see, we increased our retention from $5 million to $10 million. Therefore, the $600,000 increase is even more than it looks in that we are not purchasing the layer between $5 million and $10 million which was the most expensive. For the same coverage, the rate went from $900,000 to $2.3 million."[18]

A surprising number of physicians (estimated at 8 to 18 percent in California) are going bare,[19] meaning they are practicing without malpractice insurance. The Board of Directors of Good Samaritan Hospital in West Islip, New York, passed a resolution which required all physicians on the staff to carry malpractice insurance. Three physicians chose to "go bare," and the hospital moved to suspend their hospital privileges. Two physicians accepted their suspension, but the third obtained a temporary injunction against the hospital. A fourth physician subsequently elected to go bare and was permitted to do so by the injunction. Thus two physicians are practicing in the hospital without malpractice insurance despite a ruling adopted by the governing body of the institution.[20]

Medical discipline still leaves much to be desired in the eyes of many. A special committee of the New York State Assembly was most critical of doctors and hospitals in that state. The assembly committee accused doctors of altering medical records to protect themselves and claimed that "professional references are frequently a sham. . . . Accepted practice today enables a problem physician to move within the state when he or she loses privileges at a hospital." The committee cited hospitals for providing good references for known problem physicians when they left to go elsewhere.[21]

It was most distressing to learn from California that Dr. Nork is treating patients at a federal prison. A loophole in the law permits a physician to practice medicine in a federal facility without a California license.[22]

Debate over so-called unnecessary surgery is sure to continue. There is no questioning the fact that some elective surgery can be delayed or may not be necessary at all. However, is a second surgical opinion necessarily the right one? Surgery which might be judged unnecessary this year might prove to be necessary in the future.

The confrontation of doctors with lawyers which has been open warfare on some occasions may lessen or has lessened but realistically will always be with us, at least on those issues concerning medical malpractice. Members of both professions are usually cast on opposing sides of the argument, a doctor as the accused and the lawyer as the accuser.

Neither side should forget the most important party, the patient. Doctors, lawyers, and society as a whole must come to grips with the matter of determining if the present system of compensating victims is indeed in the best interests of the patient. It is the author's contention that it is not and that doctors and lawyers must and should be a part of the decision-making process that produces a better system.

In making the case that more legislative action is needed the author is convinced that there is no question that the present system for handling malpractice claims has been burdensome to both plaintiffs and defendants and is costly and inefficient in expeditiously directing funds to worthy claimants.

In reviewing proposed solutions, it is concluded that ceilings on awards, structured awards, and itemized awards are all approaches that may prove to be significant in the rate setting process. James Durkin, an experienced actuary in the health field, said: "Limits on awards are the single most valuable technique for cutting costs and for making actuarial projections more precise."[23]

As noted in Chapter 8, ceilings on awards have been challenged in the courts of some states, and decisions have been handed down ruling them unconstitutional. The structure of awards as an alternative to lump sum payments discussed in Chapter 7 could be helpful in stabilizing insurance premiums.

Setting a limit on damages for pain and suffering and a requirement for "itemized verdicts" in all malpractice cases proposed by the New York panel also could be helpful.

Legislation providing for introduction of information on collateral sources, or other payments made to victims, can contribute to reducing costs. The foregoing can be considered as tinkering with the present system rather than new approaches. Chief Justice Warren Burger of the U.S. Supreme Court, speaking in 1976 at a National Conference on the Causes of Popular Dissatisfaction with the Administration of Justice, suggested the following major reforms as related to medical malpractice:

> Ways must be found to provide reasonable compensation for injuries resulting from negligence of hospitals and doctors, without the distortion in the cost of medical and hospital care witnessed in the past few years. This is a high priority.
>
> Ways must be found to compensate people for injuries from negligence fo others without having the process take years to complete and consume up to half the damages awarded. The workmen's compensation statutes may be a useful guide in developing new processes and essential standards.[24]

Assemblyman Barry Keene of California, former AMA President Malcolm Todd, and Irving Lewis, staff director of New York's Special Advisory Panel on Medical Malpractice, are others who look to workmen's compensation as a better way to deal with medical malpractice. Keene said that workmen's compensation normally pays 72 percent, much more than Justice Burger said our present system provides.[25]

Irving Lewis said: "We need scheduling of awards such as workmen's compensation of Veterans' Administration Service connected disability. Is it more unfair to place a dollar amount for an award for a disability than to leave the person at the mercy of a system in which he or she may not receive anything?"[26]

Malcolm Todd, M.D., contended that "social equity requires that the artificial and arbitrary distinctions now made between those patients who suffer injury from negligence and those whose injuries are not the result of negligence be eliminated. Both patients suffer equally and justice demands that they be compensated equally."[27]

Since workmen's compensation has been operative for some time for work-related accidents, promoting such a system for medical malpractice might be easier to sell to legislators than some other approaches. In discussing a workmen's compensation system for medical malpractice, the issue of its constitutionality has been raised but it must not be forgotten that the workmen's compensation concept was originally thought to be unconstitutional.[28] The thinking of the courts changed and workmen's compensation has long since become an accepted procedure for dealing with accidents on the job.

No matter what direction we choose in trying to devise a new way to compensate malpractice victims and others injured within the health care delivery system, the key issue is to find a new way to insure the risk. Dr. Todd hit the mark when he said that "there is no way that 392,000 doctors and 7,000 hospitals can indemnify 216 million people."[29] We must broaden the base of those who pay for this insurance coverage. A proposal which seems promising is one which would develop a system of medical accident insurance that could be added to health insurance policies.

Individuals or families would carry insurance for medical accidents rather than the providers of the service. This insurance would cover those claims that are not the result of negligence or malpractice.

The federal government in conjunction with commercial carriers could inaugurate a program for the more than 200 million Americans who could purchase as much medical accident coverage as they wish or can afford. Even if the premium cost were as small as $5 or $10 per year, a pool would be available for payments to victims of medical accidents. This pool would be the first source of recovery to which victims would turn. In cases of medical malpractice, the patient and his or her family could go through the traditional route. Any money recovered could be used as an offset against the limits provided for in the insurance policy, thereby avoiding duplicate payments.

Professor Clark Havighurst of the Duke University Law School has been promoting what he calls Medical Adversity Insurance wherein the patient would buy coverage just as air travelers purchase flight insurance. Havighurst does not recommend that his Medical Adversity Insurance cover every bad result. He proposed that a list be prepared which would specify coverage for defined events.[30]

To those who would argue that it would be unfair to the patient or the consumer to add on this extra cost, one can counter that the patient and the consumer is now picking up the cost of defensive medicine and the pass through cost of increased malpractice premiums which could possibly be lessened under a new system. There seems to be little question that defensive medicine does exist and that it adds to increased health care costs, even if in some instances it might be termed "good medicine." It is not unusual for a patient to be over-tested, over-referred, and hospitalized longer than necessary. This all relates to the fear of a malpractice claim which doctors view as an attack upon professional competency and reputation.

If medical accident coverage were available, it could help to reduce malpractice claims since another route would be available for those who have been injured, whether it was a case of malpractice or a medical accident. Jurors seeing an obviously injured person before them may well think it is more important to provide an award than it is to clearly decide whether it is really a matter of malpractice.

Since very few of us are hospitalized in the course of any given year and an even smaller percent have surgery and in most instances the surgery is successful, it would seem that this would be an insurable risk. Inasmuch as this is a departure from insurance tradition, predictably carriers might scream that it cannot be done and that it is actuarily unsound. In seven years of direct contact with insurers as a legislative committee chairman, I have been appalled by the lack of initiative displayed by the insurance industry. The St. Paul with its claims made approach is one of the few companies that has shown any willingness to take action other than to leave the scene.

Joint underwriting associations, the industry's answer to the problem of continued malpractice coverage, have been totally unsuccessful in curbing rising premiums. Doctors, hospital administrators, and others who have had dealings with the JUAs have been convinced that the insurance carriers were not terribly concerned about the success or failure of JUAs once they were put into operation.

The industry which for so many years fought efforts to establish a data base on medical malpractice began to dig in its heels again in 1977 after only a few years of closed claims reports. Commissioner Lester Rawls of the Oregon Insurance Department, a leader among state regulators, was fighting desperately to continue collecting this data. Rawls said that he thinks "the insurance industry is all wrong. I agree that we may have enough statistics. We don't know however, the effects of the legislation passed or that which will be passed in the future." Rawls claimed that it takes only 15 minutes for insurance companies to fill out the statistical reports.[31]

In 1977 the insurance industry started some movement toward funding research programs which among other things would give carriers, legislators and the public a handle as to the price tag of medical no-fault, an often-discussed solution.

Professor Jeffrey O'Connell of the University of Illinois was the leading advocate of adopting a no-fault approach for medical services. O'Connell with Robert Keeton fathered the no-fault concept for automobile insurance.

In his book *Ending Insult to Injury* O'Connell states his case for medical no-fault:

> Elective no-fault liability may thus make especially good sense for the medical profession as well as for pharmaceutical houses. Unquestionably, there are medical procedures which give rise to adverse but expectable results regardless of fault but which nonetheless often lead to medical malpractice claims. For many such procedures it would make sense to allow health care providers to elect to pay out-of-pocket loss automatically when those adverse results happen. Areas of anesthesia, neurosurgery, orthopedics, and certain side effects from drugs, for example, come immediately to mind. It is not without significance that doctors—abhorring the stigma of malpractice suits—have been advocating no-fault insurance payments covering medical injuries. Keep in mind, too, that the stunning success of no-fault auto insurance in allowing more people to be eligible for payment, while at the same time stabilizing and even reducing insurance premiums, is going to greatly increase the receptivity of all kinds of enterprises—medical and otherwise—to experimentation with no-fault insurance.[32]

The wisdom of experimenting with no-fault insurance for injuries incurred in the course of medical treatment is echoed by the Final Report of the HEW Secretary's Commission on Medical Malpractice.

O'Connell reported that three of the largest hospitals in the Midwest and one of the biggest health insurers in that area were speaking seriously in mid-1977 of a pilot program to determine the feasibility of medical no-fault. The California Tort Reform Commission also gave medical no-fault serious consideration. O'Connell said that people want assurance of payment. He pointed out that preparing for and going to trial and undergoing cross-examination is a very unhappy experience for most people.[33] The same argument could be used just as forcefully in support of a workmen's compensation system.

Although automobile no-fault has been successful in speeding up payment of claims, it has many critics. Complaints from those states having no-fault indicate that savings are elusive and costs are still uncontrolled.

A no-fault plan in the health field could be devastating. Under the existing medical liability program, doctors and hospitals must carry insurance. The patient relies upon the providers coverage without any obligation to pay an insurance premium. If the patient is allowed to bring an action for every disappointment in the health delivery system, it could be catastrophic in terms of health care costs.

It seems unlikely that the reduction in litigation costs would be sufficient to finance the resultant influx of claims and awards that medical no-fault would bring.

Keeton, himself, splits with O'Connell on the question of the applicability of no-fault to medical services. Medical no-fault, Keeton said, "would lead to only slight improvement in efficiency and to substantially higher costs."[34]

Arbitration, another departure from the time-honored manner of handling malpractice, is being tried in many states. Arbitration on a limited scale in southern California has had some success. A program was started in July 1969 in eight California hospitals. The American Arbitration Association reported that administration costs in those hospitals dropped from $1,000 to $100 per closed claim. At the same time, eight other non-participating hospitals in the same area saw their figures rise from $498 to $1,000 per closed claim.[35]

Arbitration might be quite useful in settling small claims. Robert E. Cartwright, past-president of the Association of Trial Lawyers of America, said: "In a lot of malpractice cases, where maybe the damages are only $5,000 to $10,000 you [the lawyer] just have to turn the people down, even though they have a good case. Now we suggest that type of case be handled by arbitration, because it is faster, it is more economical to process, and we think that might eliminate that particular problem."[36]

For the most part, voluntary binding arbitration has been the form of arbitration adopted by state legislatures. Its proponents feel that the plaintiff's desire for a speedy settlement to a claim would encourage swifter settlements which would help all parties involved rather than prolonged courtroom proceedings. Opponents argue that every arbitrated case which has a decision unsatisfactory to either party would certainly lead to a subsequent jury trial, thereby adding to the cost and delaying disposition of malpractice cases. It will take many years to adequately judge the effectiveness of arbitration as is the problem with virtually all of the legislative solutions enacted since 1975.

National health insurance is seen by some as another promising solution. Ludlam is among its supporters, outlining several ways that national health insurance could conceivably deal with malpractice. In the offing for many years, national health insurance could (1) provide for further study on medical malpractice; (2) require that collateral source or duplicate payments be considered with respect to hospitals; (3) require recovery on a schedule of payments which could limit attorneys' fees; (4) remove malpractice from the present tort system; (5) provide excess insurance coverage which has become a problem for hospitals; and (6) provide for full assumption of malpractice insurance costs by the federal government.[37]

It is quite possible that national health insurance could hurt rather than help the medical malpractice problem. The author's reservations about national health insurance being a way out of the malpractice issue are shared by John A. Wadlewski, vice-president of Argonaut Insurance Company. Wadlewski, in a letter to Senator Edward M. Kennedy, said:

> It would seem logical that under a national health insurance program, the number of patients or people seeking medical help would increase and with an increase in patients, it would seem that the potential for claims increases. In the light of more claims, it would seem that ratio should go upward.
>
> Under a national health program, the per doctor patient load may also increase and this could create a need for haste in treatment, in turn creating potential claims.
>
> We feel that the increased utilization of medical treatment

which would result from a national health insurance plan would result in an increase in malpractice claims and costs.[38]

Wadlewski, however, sees some benefits under national health insurance. He continued: "On the other hand, it should be kept in mind that a patient may be irritated to the point of suit because of high bills and persistent dunning for delinquent payments. Free medical service may eliminate this source of irritation and to the degree that it does, may reduce frequency of claims or at least suits."

This has not been the experience under Medicare and Medicaid, and there is little evidence to lead one to expect that patients' attitudes will change under national health insurance.

For years, the federal government's role in medical malpractice was one of mainly financing studies. When Caspar Weinberger was secretary of Health, Education and Welfare, he said: "Medical malpractice insurance, like professional licensure is a state responsibility."[39] Appropriate answers to malpractice should be found at the state level. Separate action by legislatures in our fifty states in effect have created fifty different demonstration projects. These projects can test the worth of many proposals that have been put forth as solutions. It is possible that steps that could correct the situation in one state would not be feasible or workable in another jurisdiction.

Governor Otis R. Bowen, M.D., of Indiana said that "from the potential field of fifty different possibilities, the ultimate answers to the malpractice dilemma will be found. Then the best solution can be applied on a nationwide basis. This is the federal system at its best." Bowen was frank to admit that his state's much-hailed solution may not be the only solution or the best solution. In fact, "we all must steel ourselves for the possibility that ours may ultimately prove to have been no solution at all."[40]

Thomas C. Jones, Commissioner of Insurance for the State of Michigan, and Bernzweig are among those who see medical malpractice as part of a greater insurance issue—compensating injured victims. Jones claimed that personal injury compensation is inadequate. There are problems, he said for persons buying insurance such as doctors and hospitals who have had to go outside the traditional framework to buy insurance, and by persons filing claims. Commissioner Jones maintained that "it is not a medical malpractice issue or a products liability issue, it is really an injury compensation issue."[41]

Bernzweig said that "we are dealing with products liability, auto liability, workmen's compensation etc. I am not sure that private carriers can adequately deal with this total picture since we seem to go from one liability insurance crisis to another."[42] Bernzweig called for a national policy on injury reparations for all categories of victims:

> It is a constant source of amazement that the generic nature of all injury-compensation problems has received so little attention in this country. Interested persons have been treated in one categorical study after another, each dealing with its particular subject matter as though it were somehow unrelated to all the other problem areas. At the federal level study commissions and task forces have looked at worker's compensation, automobile reparations, medical malpractice, products liability, injuries to human research subjects and injuries to persons who receive vaccines under national immunization programs. . . . The number and variety of high-level studies devoted to one aspect or another of the injury-compensation issue is eloquent testimony to the fact that there is no coordinated national policy on this critical matter. Until there is one, it may be expected that the collective problems of each punitive compensation system will further exacerbate.
>
> Bear in mind that from the vantage point of the injured person, the economic consequences of his injury are far more important than the classification of its cause; yet, with the greatest of specificity, the present reparations system neatly divides claimants into categories and makes their ability to receive compensation entirely dependent on how they were injured or where they were injured. It is submitted that these should not be the determinative issues and that a more rational approach to injury reparations can and must be devised.[43]

Municipal liability and liability insurance for lawyers are added starters to this list of insurance problems. With lawyers themselves beginning to feel the crunch of liability insurance, it is quite possible that the bar might be more favorably disposed to solutions that they formerly fought.

There are strong indications that the general public may be more willing to accept far-reaching changes with respect to medical malpractice than are legislators and competing special interest groups. Several polls—including the Gallup Poll and the New York Daily News Poll—show widespread support for significant changes (see Tables 12 and 13).

Converting public opinion into legislative action is not easy,

Table 12

GALLUP POLL

1,626 adults were surveyed between May 30 and June 2, 1975

85 percent for stronger disciplining of doctors by the medical profession

89 percent for a schedule of attorneys' fees for malpractice cases

90 percent were aware of strikes and work slowdowns by doctors in California and New York

62 percent for placing a dollar ceiling to be placed on jury awards in malpractice cases

59 percent favored a five-year statute of limitations

57 percent for taking malpractice suits out of courts and placing them in the hands of an arbitration panel or committee

Source: "Gallup Finds Public Backs Move to Remove Incompetent Doctors," *New York Times,* June 15, 1975.

Table 13

DAILY NEWS POLL

533 persons interviewed in New Jersey and New York
on July 9, 10, 11, 1975

62 percent opposed doctors' strikes and slowdowns to protest increases in malpractice premiums

68 percent for placing a limit on malpractice awards as a means of cutting down malpractice insurance costs

81 percent for support for limiting lawyers fees in malpractice cases

Source: Harry Stathos, "Docs' Insurance Strike Raised Public's Temperature, Poll Finds," *New York Daily News,* August 11, 1975.

particularly with a controversial issue such as medical malpractice. The high percentage of lawyers within legislatures and the effectiveness of trial lawyers as lobbyists are among the deterrents to action such as that supposedly backed by the general public.

The problems encountered by legislators considering the medical malpractice issue were graphically outlined by Assemblyman Keene of California before a national conference of legislators:

> Prepare to deal with people who will tell you it is a doctor's problem, failing to recognize that costs are passed on to the patient; with people who are willing to consume your every energy searching for a villain when there is none; with people who have the magic solution when in reality they lack basic knowledge of the subject matter and are simply re-inventing the wheel; with people who have very narrow point of views related to their own particular discipline; with people who demand an iron-clad guarantee of the fact that you have the solution; with people who will try to blackjack you into a response; and finally with people who may be totally unappreciative of your efforts in their behalf.[44]

As long as health care is rendered on this earth, legislators, lawyers, patients, health care providers, and others must be concerned with the quality of that care and protection for persons injured while receiving care. The perfect solution to medical malpractice and medical injury does not exist because just as we are fallible beings there will always be acts of medical malpractice and medical injury.

If we are to find a better way to insure the malpractice risk, however, we must speed up resolution of malpractice claims for the benefit of victims as well as defendants, and if we are to effectively and expeditiously discipline medical professionals, all parties must be ready to compromise conflicting points of view. In legislative circles, the best bill is usually one that everyone can find fault with because in controversial matters, corrective legislation must involve give and take by all.

We cannot afford for long to leave the malpractice issue unattended. If left alone, it is a time-bomb that could threaten the stability of our nation's entire health care delivery system.

California Medical Malpractice Insurance Data, by Company

AMERICAN MUTUAL (NORTHERN CALIFORNIA)
Limits up to $100,000/$300,000

Policy Year	(1) Premium Collected	(2) Incurred Losses Reported	(3) Incurred Losses Developed	(4) Loss Ratio (3) ÷ (1)
1963	$ 1,683,783	$ 1,914,514	$ 1,914,514	113.7%
1964	1,814,670	2,676,744	2,676,744	147.5
1965	1,907,980	2,938,769	2,938,769	154.0
1966	2,378,150	4,382,029	5,336,881	224.4
1967	2,744,503	5,873,733	7,117,554	259.3
1968	4,343,472	5,234,183	7,217,429	166.2
1969	7,299,283	6,556,003	10,332,445	141.6
1970	10,779,521	8,061,169	19,702,927	182.8
1971	12,104,238	5,803,263	22,142,385	182.9
1972	12,072,000	2,572,222	17,301,277	143.3
TOTAL	$57,127,600	$46,012,629	$96,680,925	169.2%

Source: State of California Insurance Department, Sacramento, 1975.

ARGONAUT (NORTHERN CALIFORNIA & NEVADA)
All Limits as of 12/31/74

	(1)	(2)	(3)	(4)
		Incurred Losses		
Occurrence Year	Premium Earned	Reported	Developed	Loss Ratio (3) ÷ (1)
1973	$ 6,165,876	$4,276,241	$13,291,845	215.6%
1974	5,215,588	1,143,226	11,939,281	228.9
TOTAL	$11,381,464	$5,410,467	$25,231,126	221.7%

CNA (SAN DIEGO & RIVERSIDE COUNTIES)
All Limits as of 12/31/74

	(1)	(2)	(3)	(4)
		Incurred Losses		
Occurrence Year	Premium Earned	Reported	Developed	Loss Ratio (3) ÷ (1)
1970	$ 49,000	$ 127,000	$ 149,000	304.1%
1971	1,738,000	1,621,000	2,026,000	116.6
1972	1,915,000	1,022,000	1,572,000	82.1
1973	2,189,000	1,182,000	2,627,000	120.0
1974	2,242,000	830,000	5,533,000	246.8
TOTAL	$8,133,000	$4,782,000	$11,907,000	146.4%

HARTFORD ACCIDENT & INDEMNITY (SOUTHERN CALIFORNIA)
All Limits

	(1)	(2)	(3)	(4)
		Incurred Losses		
Occurrence Year	Premium Earned	Reported	Developed	Loss Ratio (3) ÷ (1)
1970	$ 2,625,085	$ 4,915,311	$ 5,782,719	220.3%
1971	13,806,635	18,732,204	23,415,255	169.6
1972	15,634,326	21,775,061	33,500,094	214.3
1973	17,436,036	18,333,245	40,740,544	233.7
TOTAL	$49,502,082	$63,755,821	$103,438,612	209.0%

PACIFIC INDEMNITY (SOUTHERN CALIFORNIA)
All Limits

Policy Year	(1) Premium Collected	(2) Incurred Losses Reported	(3) Incurred Losses Developed	(4) Loss Ratio (3) ÷ (1)
1963	$ 2,118,276	$ 3,013,610	$ 3,013,610	142.3%
1964	2,478,105	4,551,171	4,551,171	183.7
1965	2,728,604	5,594,108	5,594,108	205.0
1966	3,319,832	7,762,236	7,712,968	232.3
1967	4,846,717	10,187,949	12,314,223	254.1
1968	7,800,384	11,004,874	15,099,404	193.6
1969	14,854,420	15,541,040	24,271,255	163.4
1970	11,313,714	7,772,583	13,411,216	118.5
1971	2,029,884	1,589,323	3,327,222	163.9
1972	2,182,080	1,279,762	5,315,987	243.6
TOTAL	$53,672,016	$68,296,656	$94,611,164	176.3%

TRAVELERS (NORTHERN & SOUTHERN CALIFORNIA)
All Limits as of 12/31/74

Occurrence Year	(1) Premium Earned	(2) Incurred Losses Reported	(3) Incurred Losses Developed	(4) Loss Ratio (3) ÷ (1)
1974	$29,843,402	$9,447,992	$62,986,613	211.1%

Column (1) represents the earned portion of premiums collected segregated by calendar year.

Column (2) represents the value as of 12/31/74 of claims reported by year claim occurred and makes no provision for possible changes in value of reported claims which have not yet been settled or for late reported claims.

Column (3) represents developed (ultimate) losses for the respective years in which the claims occurred.

Column (4) represents the ratio of developed losses by occurrence year to the calendar year earned premium.

·◌[Appendix B]◌·

All-Industry Committee Special Malpractice Review 1974 Closed Claim Survey

IN NOVEMBER OF 1976, the All-Industry Committee released the results of its Special Malpractice Review: a survey of closed claims for the Year 1974.

Some of the findings are as follows: Of the claims against doctors about one-third (34%) were against surgeons or surgery-related specialists classified as "high risk" by insurers for rating purposes, although this class comprised only 17% of insured doctors. (High-risk specialists include neurosurgeons, obstetricians, orthopedists, plastic surgeons, and anesthesiologists.)

Of the total number of claims for which a payment was made, 74% was paid on behalf of doctors, 19% on behalf of hospitals, and 7% on behalf of dentists and other health care providers.

The actual average claim payment to all successful plaintiffs was almost $25,000 ($24,907). Among the various classifications of insureds, the range of average claim payments varied from a high of $32,810 for "low-risk" surgeons to a low of $10,387 for dentists and other miscellaneous categories. Claim payments on behalf of hospitals averaged $16,758.

The average length of time from the occurrence of a medical incident to the resolution of a resulting claim was thirty-one months. Seven years elapsed before 96% of the incidents producing claim payments were closed.

The study suggests that reducing the statute of limitations to three years in all states might eliminate some of the claims and claim dollars. A precise estimate of the overall effect of such a change, however, is not possible since it is quite likely that if the statute of limitations were shortened, claim reporting patterns would accelerate, thus minimizing the potential reduction in claims and claims dollars. Shortening the statute of limitations would, however, facilitate more equitable pricing which would ultimately benefit both insureds and insurers alike.

147

Many reported claims do involve major injuries that are not, however, caused by malpractice. Modern medicine practiced perfectly cannot prevent some injuries, nor can it always cure the seriously injured or diseased.

Over half the incidents on which claim payments were made produced a payment of less than $10,000. These accounted for less than 5% of total claim payment dollars and less than 15% of total economic loss. At the other end of the scale, fewer than 10% of the incidents involved payments over $100,000 but produced 66% of total claim payment dollars and 49% of the economic loss.

Major Conclusions of the Michigan Crisis Committee Survey, 1975

1. "The plaintiff's bar has contributed to the malpractice crisis by filing an exceptionally large number of malpractice cases since the advent of no fault automobile insurance." (Malpractice claims which increased at an average of 23 percent a year from 1970 through 1973 increased by 61 percent in 1974, the first full year after passage of Michigan's no fault automobile insurance legislation.)

2. "Very few cases ever get to the jury. Most are settled by lawyers for a variety of reasons, many of which have little or nothing to do with 'merit.' . . . More than four out of every five medical malpractice cases never go to trial."

3. "A rational settlement negotiation process may be distorted by the fact that a small group of attorneys regularly decide between them a disproportionately high number of medical malpractice cases. . . . The system encourages counsel, particularly the specialist who wants to survive, to commence and carry out negotiations which, by tacit agreement, result in settlements that accommodate the other's professional and economic needs. The final product of the 'system' is to achieve recovery through the process of compromise for the vast majority of plaintiffs."

4. "In more than four out of every five medical malpractice cases, money is awarded the plaintiff. . . . Doctors understand quite clearly that significant proportions of these settled cases do not involve clearcut physician negligence . . . but merely a bad or unexpected medical result over which the doctor has no control. Medicine believes it is actually underwriting the cost of a 'no fault system,' while being blamed professionally by the public for a level of fault which has simply not been proven."

5. "A few attorneys have a tremendous economic stake in the present court-jury litigation system for medical malpractice."

149

6. "The high volume plaintiff's counsel in medical malpractice cases sue for higher damages, sue slightly more defendants per cases, and take much longer to conclude each case than other attorneys."

7. "More stringent reporting requirements, and greater regulatory control over malpractice insurance carriers is needed. . . . The most cursory analysis of the hospital and doctor defendants in the cases filed during the Survey point up the need for insurance companies to report and publish a far broader spectrum of information regarding the records of their insurers. Such information is now almost impossible to obtain."

·𝕴 Appendix D 𝕴·

Summary of Recommendations
of the HEW Secretary's Commission
on Medical Malpractice

DEFENSIVE MEDICINE

THE COMMISSION finds that defensive medicine is the alteration of modes of medical practice, induced by the threat of liability, for the principal purposes of forestalling the possibility of lawsuits by patients as well as providing a good legal defense in the event such lawsuits are instituted.

The Commission recommends that over-utilization of health-care resources by any provider should be aggressively attacked by physician-directed regulatory efforts. Hospital utilization committees should be mandatory in every hospital, and their efficiency should be subject to statistical analysis and review by physician-directed supervisory groups.

In order to encourage physicians to render the highest possible quality care and to reduce the practice of unwarranted defensive medicine the Commission recommends that medical and osteopathic organizations exert maximum moral suasion over physicians who avoid professional responsibilities on the basis of fear of malpractice liability.

GOOD SAMARITANS

The Commission finds that there is no factual basis for the commonly-asserted belief that malpractice suits are likely to stem from rendering emergency care at the scene of accidents.

The Commission recommends that widespread publicity be given to this fact in order to allay the fears of physicians, nurses, and other health-care providers in this regard and to encourage the rendering of aid in non-hospital emergency situations.

151

QUALIFIED IMMUNITY

The Commission recommends that the states enact legislation to provide qualified immunity to hospitals and members of hospital rescue teams while they are attempting to resuscitate any person who is in immediate danger of loss of life, provided good faith is exercised.

The Commission recommends that the states enact legislation designed to provide qualified immunity to physicians and other health-care personnel who respond to emergencies arising from unexpected complications that arise in the course of medical treatment rendered by other physicians or other health-care personnel.

The Commission recommends that all physicians who regularly practice in hospitals be encouraged, through continuing medical education, to become proficient in cardiac arrest and cardiopulmonary resuscitation techniques.

ALLIED HEALTH PERSONNEL

The Commission finds that there does not appear to be any indication that the use of allied health-care personnel, particularly registered nurses and technicians, where properly qualified or supervised, has led to any significant problems of medical malpractice liability or malpractice insurance coverage. Where the use of such allied health-care personnel is medically justified, it has not been shown that malpractice problems have significantly restrained their use.

MEDIA

The Commission finds that despite isolated instances of emotionalism, bias and inaccuracy, press, radio and television coverage of medical malpractice cases and problems is, on the whole, straightforward, factual, and balanced.

PATIENT INJURIES

The Commission finds that patient injuries, real or imagined, are prime factors in the malpractice problem.

LEGAL DOCTRINES

The Commission finds that some courts have applied certain legal doctrines for the purpose of creating or relieving the liability of health professionals.

The Commission further finds that such special doctrines, or the application thereof, are no longer justified.

INFORMED CONSENT

The Commission finds that the doctrine of informed consent is subject to abuse when it imposes an unreasonable responsibility upon the physician.

RES IPSA LOQUITUR

The Commission finds that the doctrine of res ipsa loquitur in its classical sense performs a useful purpose in common law, but that it should not be applied differently in medical malpractice cases than in other types of tort litigation.

APPLICATION OF LEGAL DOCTRINES

The Commission recommends that legal doctrines relating to the liability of health professionals should be applied in the same manner as they are applied to all classes of defendants, whether they be favorable or unfavorable to health professional defendants. Such doctrines would include (a) the application of the discovery rule under the statute of limitations; (b) the terms of the statute of limitations; (c) the application of the doctrine of res ipsa loquitur to injuries arising in the performance of professional services; (d) the rule allowing liability based on oral guarantee of good results, and (e) the doctrine of informed consent to treatment.

RESTATEMENT OF MEDICAL-LEGAL PRINCIPLES

The Commission believes the time has come to develop greater logic, consistency, and uniformity in the medical-legal rules and doctrines affecting the delivery of health-care, and therefore recommends that all such medical-legal rules and doctrines be clarified and made uniform in application throughout the United States. In order to achieve this objective, the Commission recommends that a broad-based group, representing all segments of the health-care system, the legal profession, and the general public, be convened to develop the appropriate definitions and guidelines in the nature of a Restatement of the Law of Medical-Legal Principles.

·CONTINGENT FEE

The Commission recommends that courts adopt appropriate rules and that all states enact legislation requiring a uniform graduated scale of contingent fee rates in all medical malpractice litigation. The contingent fee scale should be one in which the fee rate decreases as the recovery amount increases.

DEFENSE COSTS

Realizing that the matter of defense costs is an important element in the cost of malpractice insurance, the Commission recommends that a method of minimizing these costs be studied.

LEGAL AID

The Commission recommends that public legal assistance mechanisms be established, or expanded where they already exist, to assure adequate legal representation to persons with small malpractice claims.

MEDICAL-LEGAL COOPERATION

The Commission recommends that the professions of law and medicine seek to improve their level of understanding and cooperation, specifically in the area of malpractice litigation to facilitate the handling of claims in the most equitable manner.

EXPERT TESTIMONY

The Commission recommends that organized medicine and osteopathy establish an official policy encouraging members of their professions to cooperate fully in medical malpractice actions so that justice will be assured for all parties; and the Commission encourages the establishment of pools from which expert witnesses can be drawn.

NOTICE OF INTENT TO FILE SUIT

The Commission recommends that state laws be amended to require that a written notice of intent to file a malpractice suit be given to the potential defendant within a specific time period prior to the running of the statute of limitations. Upon the filing of such notice, the statute of limitations would be automatically extended for a specified period, to enable the parties to negotiate an amicable settlement in good faith.

AD DAMNUM

The Commission recommends that the states enact legislation eliminating inclusion of dollar amounts in ad damnum clauses in malpractice suits.

INSURANCE AVAILABILITY

The Commission finds that malpractice insurance is currently available to health-care practitioners under group plans and the market for such insurance is competitive. Malpractice insurance is also available to individual health-care practitioners, although they appear to have more difficulty in locating insurance sources. Umbrella and excess coverage are also available both to individuals and under group plans.

INSURANCE CONTINGENCY PLAN

The Commission recommends that the insurance industry and health-care provider groups work together to develop a contingency plan to provide medical malpractice insurance in the event such insurance becomes unavailable through normal market channels.

REINSURANCE

The Commission finds that to the extent that medical malpractice insurance is available in the primary market, it is available in the reinsurance market.

INSURANCE FOR FREE CLINICS

The Commission recommends that the free clinic movement consider medical malpractice insurance necessary protection for patients and health-care personnel. To assist in remedying this situation, the Commission recommends that governmental authorities consider the overall need for medical malpractice insurance and its cost in evaluating applications for grants to free clinics, not just the need for coverage of the activities covered by the grant.

RATE MAKING

The Commission finds that the present methods for establishing malpractice insurance rates, including groupings of physicians and institutions for rating purposes, may not be equitable for all providers or in the best interests of the public.

RATING CLASSIFICATIONS

The Commission finds that health-care providers by encouraging numerous separate specialty rating classifications have contributed to the establishment of a rating classification program which may be inequitable to some practitioners and which under some circumstances may adversely affect the cost and availability of professional liability insurance.

The Commission recommends that the American Medical Association, American Osteopathic Association, American Nursing Association, American Dental Association and the American Hospital Association meet with the leaders of the insurance industry to study alternative methods of classifying individual practitioners and institutions for rate making purposes; for example: on a group basis to the medical staff of a hospital or to a county society.

RATING HOSPITALS

The Commission recommends that serious consideration be given to establishing level premium rates for hospitals within a distinct area based on the number of beds and/or out-patient visits.

STATISTICAL REPORTING

The Commission finds that inadequacies in the collection and analysis of appropriate data have precluded the development of sound actuarial practices and rates, and that state insurance departments are generally inadequately equipped to monitor effectively the rate making process employed in establishing malpractice insurance rates.

The Commission recommends that the National Association of Insurance Commissioners work with the insurance industry to establish a uniform statistical reporting system for medical malpractice insurance and that data be reported to a single data collection agent who will compile it, validate it and make it available to state insurance regulators, carriers and other interested users.

MARKETING MALPRACTICE INSURANCE

The Commission recommends that the insurance industry develop improved channels of communication concerning the marketing, economics and quality of medical malpractice insurance so that responsible sources of medical malpractice insurance are more widely known to health-care providers, insurance brokers, and independent insurance agents.

INSURANCE SERVICES

The Commission recommends that purchasers of medical malpractice insurance, especially associations and institutions, give due regard to the loss prevention and claims handling capabilities of prospective insurance carriers and that active programs be instituted and encouraged in cooperation with insurance carriers designed to prevent the occurrence of injury as well as to assist in disposing of meritorious cases as quickly and as fairly as possible.

The Commission recommends that states require insurers issuing medical malpractice policies to disclose loss prevention and claims settlement practices on request by purchasers and in any sales promotional material distributed to prospective purchasers.

MEDICARE

The Commission recommends that Congress and the Secretary of HEW review those portions of Title 18 of the Social Security Act (Medicare) which contain benefit payment restrictions and other limitations that impede patient rapport and, which may tend to increase the number of malpractice claims. The Commission urges re-evaluation of Title 18 so that patient frustrations are reduced to the extent feasible.

The Commission recommends the launching of an educational and public relations program aimed at Medicare participants in order to increase understanding of the program's statutory limitations and to decrease public dissatisfaction and frustration which may lead to malpractice claims.

The Commission recognizes the need to measure and evaluate the impact of malpractice claims and litigation on the costs of Medicare and other Federally-supported health-care programs and the Commission therefore recommends that appropriate studies be initiated to achieve that objective. Such analysis should include not only the premiums involved but the cost of handling the claims and the costs to other Federally-sponsored programs that may also be providing benefits to medically injured persons.

NATIONAL HEALTH INSURANCE

The Commission recommends that new third party payment proposals, such as national health insurance, have benefit structures which are easily understood by patients and providers and that the administration of such plans be as simple as possible to avoid, to the extent possible, retroactive denials of claims and other administrative impediments which might exacerbate the patient-provider relationship and create an environment conducive to disputes, claims, and suits.

OVERLAPPING BENEFITS

The Commission recommends that an indepth analysis be made to identify the cost of overlapping health insurance benefits and to identify methods of using these resources to assure more complete coverage to all. No new Federal or Federally-funded program should be initiated without taking these factors into considerations, and all existing programs should be reviewed to achieve these objectives.

LICENSURE

The Commission finds that the competence of individual providers of health-care affects the overall quality of care. The Commission also finds that most State medical practice acts do not have adequate provisions for disciplining practitioners who have been found incompetent.

The Commission recommends that all State medical practice acts include specific authority to State licensing bodies to suspend or revoke licenses for professional incompetence.

RE-REGISTRATION OF HEALTH-CARE PROVIDERS

The Commission recommends that the states revise their licensure laws, as appropriate, to enable their licensing boards to require periodic re-registration to physicians, dentists, nurses and other health professionals, based upon proof of participation in approved continuing medical education.

EXPEDITING SANCTIONS

The Commission recommends that the States enact legislation which limits the duration of judicial ex parte stay orders to the minimum period necessary to hold an adversary hearing in cases of suspension or revocation of the licenses of health professionals by State Boards. The adversary hearing should be given priority on any court docket.

REHABILITATION OF PRACTITIONERS

The Commission recommends that State licensing laws emphasize rehabilitation of practitioners who have been found guilty of infractions.

The Commission recommends that State Boards of medical and osteopathic examiners be authorized to prescribe a range of intermediate disciplinary actions in addition to suspension or revocation of licenses, such as requiring remedial education.

NATIONWIDE STANDARDS

The Commission recommends that a feasibility study be made regarding the establishment of uniform national procedures for examining and licensing health professionals and the establishment of uniform standards of practice.

RE-CERTIFICATION OF PHYSICIANS

The Commission recommends that specialty boards periodically reevaluate and recertify physicians they have certified.

PUBLIC SCRUTINY

The Commission recommends that all state boards of medical examiners include lay members.

The Commission recommends that all disciplinary hearings be open to the public.

INSTITUTIONAL LICENSURE

The Commission recommends that studies be made to determine the impact on the quality of care of institutional and organizational licensure for allied health personnel (other than registered nurses) as an alternative to individual licensure.

STAFF PRIVILEGES

The Commission recommends that the States enact legislation to authorize, with due process, the appropriate committee of a hospital medical staff to suspend, revoke, or curtail the privileges of a physician or hospital staff member for good cause shown. The committee members and the hospital should have qualified immunity from suit for their acts. Notification of such actions should be forwarded to the appropriate State licensing boards.

CONTINUING EDUCATION

The Commission recommends that continuing education be directed toward known needs and that it be designed around performance criteria.

The Commission recommends that there be imposed upon the existing system of self-regulated continuing education control mechanisms which will require continuing medical education and evidence of provider proficiency.

CLINICAL PHARMACOLOGY

The Commission recommends that clinical pharmacology, that is, the teaching of actions, indications, side effects, etcetera of drugs used therapeutically be required as part of an integrated program for teaching the basics of therapeutics to all medical and nursing students and that similar attention be given to the same subjects in post-graduate and continuing medical education curricula.

USING MORE NURSES

The Commission recommends that physicians, hospitals, nursing homes and other institutions increase the number of professional nurses giving direct care to patients in the interests of better patient care and of minimizing malpractice suits.

CLINICAL EDUCATION FOR NURSES

The Commission recommends that in the interests of better patient care and of minimizing medical malpractice suits, nurses should be required to complete clinical practice courses in the areas of planning patient care, assessment of patient's problems, recording and reporting, clinical nursing procedures, working with other medical personnel, and educating patients in implementation of doctors' orders.

The Commission recommends that clinical courses which include human anatomy, psychology and human relations be required in the nursing curriculum.

INJURY PREVENTION

The Commission recommends the development of intensified medical injury prevention programs for every health-care institution in the nation, such programs to be predicated on the following:

1. investigation and analysis of the frequency and causes of the general categories and specific types of adverse incidents causing injuries to patients;

2. development of appropriate measures to minimize the risk of injuries and adverse incidents to patients through the cooperative efforts of all persons involved in the providing of patient care in such institutions.

QUALITY CONTROL

The Commission recommends that institutional quality control mechanisms of all types be constantly evaluated and, where proven desirable, modified so that the information they generate can be fed into a nationwide information system and into continuing education programs.

LOSS PREVENTION

The Commission finds that where genuine cooperation and support of insurance company loss-prevention programs can be achieved, a meaningful reduction in patient injuries can also be achieved.

The Commission finds that loss-prevention activities generally are limited to group plans. For the most part, activities aimed toward the individual practitioner have been minimal. There is a need for intensified loss-prevention efforts on the part of the medical malpractice insurance industry working with health-care providers and the consumer community.

The Commission recommends that the medical malpractice insurance industry develop sophisticated loss-prevention programs based on both injury and claims prevention techniques. This development will require the active participation of the provider and consumer community.

The Commission recommends that a portion of the premium dollar for institutional medical malpractice insurance be specifically identified and allocated towards loss-prevention. Health-care providers should implement and monitor the loss-prevention programs developed in cooperation with their insurance carriers.

The Commission recommends that medical malpractice carriers provide analyses of incidents to institutional health-care providers in order to aid the institutions' injury prevention programs.

NATIONWIDE DATA COLLECTION

The Commission recommends that health-care providers, consumers, attorneys, and the insurance industry form a consortium to collect and report information relating to medical injuries and medical malpractice to a Federal or Federally-sponsored data-gathering service.

It is further recommended that the Secretary of Health, Education, and Welfare convene representatives of these groups (1) to determine the kind of data needed, and (2) through existing data facilities in HEW, to work with private industry to develop the information.

INDIVIDUAL PRIVACY

The Commission recommends that the Congress, by appropriate legislation, confer privacy to the raw data collected for a nationwide medical malpractice data system comparable to the privacy that has already been accorded to data collected by the Social Security Administration and the Internal Revenue Service.

FEDERAL ASSISTANCE

The Commission recommends Federal sponsorship of research and demonstration programs in order to develop the recommended injury prevention programs. The Federal Government should also support the development of a nationwide system for the continuous monitoring and evaluation of medical injury prevention measures, in order to assure the cross-fertilization of new techniques and approaches between and among all categories of health-care providers.

HUMAN RELATIONS TRAINING

The Commission recommends that all medical, dental, and nursing schools develop and require participation in programs which integrate training in the psychological and psychosocial aspects of patient care with the physical and biological sciences.

The Commission recommends that all categories of health-care personnel receive training in order to develop attitudes and skills in the interpersonal aspects of patient care. This training should utilize the most advanced educational technology and should be included in post-graduate and continuing education programs as well as throughout the entire period of undergraduate training.

The Commission recommends that staff conferences be expanded to include discussion of the ethical, social, and psychological aspects of patient care, and that periodic faculty-student seminars be devoted exclusively to discussion of these matters.

IMPROVING THE HEALTH-CARE ENVIRONMENT

The Commission recommends that improvements be made in the physical environment and methods of management of hospitals and other health-care facilities to assure greater attention to the psychological and psychosocial needs of patients.

EDUCATION OF THE PUBLIC

The Commission recommends that special programs be developed to educate the public on health-care subjects about which patient knowledge is deficient, and which may contribute to later malpractice litigation. These subjects should include: health and hygiene (including the origins of disease, function of the body organs, nutrition needs, etc.); how to communicate with health-care personnel; the economics of medical care; the conventions of medical practice (e.g., consultation, referrals, use of surgical assistants, etc.); and the limitations of medical science.

The Commission recommends continuing programs of research and analysis aimed at increasing knowledge and understanding of patients' psychological and psychosocial needs and that findings of such research be translated into specific action programs aimed at improving the physical design and methods of management of health-care facilities and at improving the training of health-care personnel in the human relations aspects of patient care.

PATIENTS' RIGHTS

The Commission recommends that hospitals and other health-care facilities adopt and distribute statements of patients' rights in a manner which most effectively communicates these rights to all incoming patients.

TEACHING HOSPITALS

The Commission recommends that the functions of teaching hospitals be explained to all patients entering such hospitals, and that these functions be emphasized in other forms of consumer education.

SOCIO-ECONOMIC DISTINCTIONS

The Commission recommends that where they exist, distinctions in the treatment of patients in teaching hospitals based on the patient's race or socioeconomic status be eliminated.

INFORMED CONSENT

The Commission finds that there is a generally recognized right of a patient to be told about the danger inherent in proposed medical treatment. That right is consistent with the nature of the doctor-patient relationship and with fundamental fairness. A much greater degree of communication between health-care providers and patients is really good, basic medical practice and should be encouraged.

The Commission finds that the law relating to the nature of information which the health-care provider must supply to obtain valid consent for treatment is presently in flux. Adoption of uniform standards requiring full disclosure of material risks would eliminate much confusion as to the basis and nature of informed consent. Under such standards, both patient and doctor would gain a clearer understanding of their respective rights and obligations.

The Commission recommends that a responsible member of the patient's family be given appropriate explanations where the physician is justifiably reluctant to explain such matters directly to the patient because of his concern that the explanation itself is likely to have an adverse effect on the patient.

ACCESS TO MEDICAL RECORDS

The Commission finds that the unavailability of medical records without resort to litigation creates needless expense and increases the incidence of unnecessary malpractice litigation.

The Commission finds that patients have a right to the information contained in their medical records and recommends that such information be made more easily accessible to patients, and the Commission further recommends that the States enact legislation enabling patients to obtain access to the information contained in their medical records through their legal representatives, public or private, without having to file a suit.

ALTERATION OF MEDICAL RECORDS

The Commission recommends that the states enact legislation to prohibit modification, alteration, or destruction of medical records with the intent of misleading or misinforming the patient.

CLINICAL RESEARCH STANDARDS

The Commission recommends that physicians engaged in clinical research consider as minimum standards of ethical conduct the World Medical Association's Declaration of Helsinki and the American Medical Association Guidelines for Clinical Investigation.

The Commission recommends that where clinical investigation necessarily involves the participation of persons who are not legally competent to give valid consent, extraordinary precautions be established to protect the interest of such persons.

The Commission recommends that the biomedical research community make every effort to educate its prospective members in the fundamental principles of research ethics.

PROTECTION OF HUMAN SUBJECTS

The Commission recommends that the Department of Health, Education, and Welfare guidelines on medical research involving humans be applied to all persons participating in medical research regardless of the source of funds which support the investigation.

INSURANCE FOR RESEARCH SUBJECTS

The Commission recommends that whenever a grant or other funding is provided by the Federal Government for medical research involving human subjects, that the grant include a sum sufficient to provide either insurance or a self-insurance fund in order to provide compensation to any human subject who may be injured in the course of the research. Where the Federal Government itself conducts the research, precisely the same rule should apply, either through the Federal Employees' Compensation Act or other funding.

The Commission recommends that whenever research involving

human subjects is conducted by the private sector, that insurance be provided to protect against mishaps, injury, or illness directly arising out of that research.

CONSUMER INVOLVEMENT

The Commission recommends that the Secretary of Health, Education, and Welfare and the administrators of other Federally supported health-care delivery and medical research and demonstration programs establish and continue consumer involvement activities at the planning, services, supervisory, management, and coordination levels by means of board membership, advocacy and advisory mechanisms.

The Commission recommends that the same degree of consumer involvement be fostered by all appropriate non-Federal health-care delivery and research programs.

GRIEVANCE MECHANISMS

The Commission recommends that all health-care institutions establish a patient grievance mechanism capable of dealing with patient care problems.

The Commission recommends that, to the extent possible, patient grievance mechanisms be established to deal with patient care problems in non-institutional settings.

The Commission recommends that the Secretary require, as a condition of receiving Medicaid and Medicare payments, that all health-care institutions establish a patient grievance mechanism capable of dealing with direct patient care problems.

The Commission recommends the initiation of research programs to determine the best way to utilize patient grievance mechanisms to deal with problems involving patient care, including all health-care providers; hospitals, nursing homes, HMO's, clinics, and private practitioners, and also all levels of regulation—Federal, State, and professional.

STATE OFFICE OF CONSUMER HEALTH AFFAIRS

The Commission recommends that there be established in each State an Office of Consumer Health Affairs. The Commission further recommends that Federal financial assistance be made available to the States to encourage the establishment of such offices at the earliest possible date.

CLAIMS HANDLING

The Commission recommends that medical malpractice carriers develop mechanisms for improved claims handling. In particular, we recommend attention to be given to the detection and analysis of incidents having a claims potential to allow early disposition, and to further experimentation with advance medical payments.

SCREENING PANELS

The Commission recognizes the value of local efforts to mediate medical malpractice disputes, and therefore recommends continuous experimentation with voluntary mediation devices. The Commission also recommends that persons other than attorneys and members of the profession involved in the disputes be included as members of any mediation board or panel.

IMPOSED ARBITRATION

The Commission recommends more widespread use of imposed arbitration as an alternative mode for resolving small medical malpractice disputes, providing the arbitration mechanisms have the following characteristics and do not preempt contractual arbitration agreements:

1. Arbitration statutes enacted by the States should be designed to give jurisdiction over all parties, plaintiffs, and defendants, involved in a specific medical malpractice case.

2. State arbitration laws should set a maximum monetary limit for invoking the jurisdiction of the arbitration board, with cases demanding higher amounts being handled through the present jury system.

3. Arbitration panels should include some persons who are neither attorneys nor persons involved in the delivery of health-care services.

4. There should be the right of trial de novo subsequent to arbitration in the highest level jury court in the State.

5. The State arbitration statute should provide economic and legal sanctions, in order to discourage subsequent trials de novo of questionable merit, (e.g. evidentiary rules, presumptions, taxation of court costs).

6. A fairly detailed synopsis of each arbitration decision should be made and published in order to establish precedents, provide information necessary to evaluate and improve the arbitration system, and provide adequate feedback information to the health-care system.

7. Although the Commission has recommended that the results of formal arbitration proceedings be published, publicity focused on the names of parties involved in disputes should be avoided or minimized.

ENABLING LEGISLATION

The Commission recommends that all States that have not adopted legislation to make binding arbitration awards possible enact such legislation.

CONTRACTUAL ARBITRATION

The Commission finds that the utilization of contractual arbitration as an innovative method of resolving malpractice disputes is an important development that justifies continued experimentation and study prior to universal adoption.

FREEDOM OF CONTRACT

The Commission recommends that no patient be required, as a condition for receiving service, to sign an agreement requiring him to agree to arbitrate any future dispute arising out of the service.

Note: This recommendation does not apply to agreements for comprehensive health-care services in which the arbitration agreement may be a part of the overall contract for health-care services.

LAY REPRESENTATION

The Commission recommends that the panel of arbitrators include representatives from the public other than members of the professions involved in the dispute.

PUBLIC RECORD

Furthermore, the Commission recommends that the results of contractual arbitration, including the award and the basis of the award, be made a matter of public record for the purposes of study and improvement of quality of care and the avoidance of unnecessary injury to patients.

FEDERAL COERCION

The Commission is opposed in principle to any form of government activity which would induce or compel a health-care provider or a patient to agree to arbitrate disputes prior to the event which gives rise to the dispute.

ALTERNATIVE COMPENSATION SYSTEMS

The Commission recommends that the Federal Government fund one or more demonstration projects at the State or local level in order to test and evaluate the feasibility of possible alternative medical injury compensation systems.

The Commission finds that further study is warranted and essential for better definition of the event for which compensation should be paid and for developing a method of financing whatever new system is recommended.

STATE PILOT PROGRAMS

The Commission recommends that one or more State governments study and investigate, by all appropriate means, including pilot programs, the feasibility of establishing a patient injury insurance program, similar to workmen's compensation insurance, to provide designated compensation benefits for injuries arising from health-care, whether caused by medical malpractice or not.

The Commission recommends that the various proposals suggested here be developed, tested and demonstrated through both public and private initiatives, especially those which, if possible, would promptly compensate medically injured patients without regard to a finding of fault.

IMPLEMENTATION OF RECOMMENDATIONS

The Commission recommends the creation of a non-governmental, non-profit organization which would be the nationwide focal point for malpractice research, information, education, and prevention activities. The proposed organization should be broadly based and representative of the public at large, including health-care providers and third party payors, both public and private, the legal profession, insurance industry, and consumers.

Funding for this entity should come primarily from health, legal and insurance organizations, as well as from philanthropic foundations and individuals. Federal assistance could come through the research grant mechanism and the sponsorship of conferences and activities necessary to establish the organization.

Statement by
Senator Tarky Lombardi, Jr.,
Chairman, New York State
Senate Health Committee
at Public Hearing
of Secretary's Commission
on Medical Malpractice
February 25, 1972

MEDICAL MALPRACTICE has reached such crisis proportion that it is now known as the malpractice phenomenon; and the problem continues to grow.

As Chairman of the New York State Senate Committee on Health, I have had serious concern with the problem since our Committee held a major malpractice hearing in September, 1970.

At that hearing, the respected Executive Director of this Commission, Mr. Bernzweig, who was then Special Assistant in the Department of Health, Education and Welfare for Malpractice Research & Prevention, testified "there is little doubt that this nation is witnessing a level of malpractice claims and litigation unparallelled in history." Mr. Richard Bergan of the American Medical Association stated that the professional liability problem is a matter of major concern "verging on catastrophy in some areas."

All the witnesses who came before us were extremely knowledgeable —and a few had suggestions they felt would alleviate the problem. After a thorough study of the testimony received at that time, a conference was held to stimulate more definitive suggestions. Those in attendance were insurance company representatives and their attorneys, plaintiffs' attorneys, the President of our State Medical Society, representatives of the State Hospital Association, New York State Departments of Health, Education, and Insurance—which all deal with the problem—and a representative of Governor Rockefeller.

I want to emphasize that all concerned are being extremely cooperative with our Committee.

Again, everyone participating acknowledged that a major problem does exist and that the problem is becoming increasingly critical. However, the conferees still were not able to agree on what action to take toward workable solutions. The doctors and the insurance companies oppose suggestions brought forth by the plaintiffs' attorneys; these attorneys object to suggestions made by the medical profession; governmental agencies remain in a quandary.

The confusion of semantics, emphasis, definitions, and diversified viewpoints further exaggerates the malpractice problem.

HOW DO YOU CONFRONT THE MALPRACTICE CRISIS?
WHAT HAS TO BE SOLVED?

1. Is it the high cost of medical malpractice insurance?
2. Is it the unavailability of insurance to some physicians and hospitals?
3. Is it the number of malpractice claims?
4. Is it that the patient might suffer because of the reluctance of a doctor to take a risk?
5. Is it that the practice of medicine has become so sophisticated that failure is often not accepted?

While those attending the conference spoke on all these questions they could not agree on answers. I would like to address myself to some of the more valid approaches presented.

As to the high cost of medical malpractice insurance, the most visible problem in the eyes of the doctors and hospitals—WHY?

The following factors relate to the composition of high cost.

1. Lack of competition either by choice or design in selection of carriers
2. Rate setting procedures
3. Manner in which claims are handled
4. Nuisance and unfounded claims
5. The amount of compensation paid to injured patients

Insurance companies claim that writing malpractice insurance is extremely hazardous. I believe that there are only 40 carriers in the entire country presently writing malpractice business. In New York State approximately 75 percent of the malpractice coverage is written by Employers of Wausau which has contracted with the Medical Society of New York State since 1949. There are those who believe that there is a "love-in" between the carrier and the Society which may have created a quasimonopoly.

A suggestion to establish a State Insurance Fund to guarantee the availability of medical malpractice insurance was rejected by spokesmen for both the Medical Society and their insurance carrier. The Society uses medical malpractice insurance coverage as an incentive to attract members. However, the general membership has little or no voice in the Society's selection of a carrier.

Is healthy competition being stimulated by not seeking bids from other carriers either on a geographical basis or a specialty basis or a group basis?

Each year the Insurance Department approves rate increases for the carriers. Since 1966 malpractice insurance rates in New York State have risen 219 percent. The Insurance Department states that the review and approval of rates are accomplished within the same analytical framework as is used to measure past profitability. However, the Department also attempts to measure future losses and expenses. Until January 1970 this Department reviewed rate increase requests on a prior approval basis. Since then the Department has reviewed requests for rate increases on a postfiling basis. The Insurance Department does not hold public hearings prior to approving rate increases for medical malpractice coverage. Feeling that this should be changed, I have introduced legislation that is presently pending before the Insurance Committees of the Legislature that would require the Insurance Department to hold public hearings prior to approving any rate increases for medical liability insurance.

As to unavailability of medical malpractice insurance, we have found that insurance is usually available if the physician or hospital is willing to pay the price.

It appears that the number of medical malpractice claims are caused, not by the decrease in ability and efficiency of the practicing doctor today, but rather by the increase in awareness of patients as to their legal rights and remedies. Today medical news is public news and every newspaper reader becomes an instant diagnostician.

Perhaps the singly most important factor contributing to malpractice claims is the breakdown of the traditional long-term relationship between the patient and his doctor. In the present age of specialization, care is often delivered in an impersonal, hurried, fractionalized manner. Patients complain that frequently physicians display a lack of sympathy and understanding and are unconcerned about the patient's worry over his own state of health.

While patients have become more sophisticated about medical procedures, they are often unaware of the complexities and hazards of modern medical practice. They are much more prone to blame the treating physician when the final outcome is not what the patient expected or hoped for. Patient expectations are not consonant with medical reality.

Another strong influence in the decision to bring suit against a physician is the receipt of a bill which the patient regards as excessive or unjustified.

Legal specialization correlates with medical specialization. More lawyers are interested in handling malpractice cases, especially since the advent of proposed New York State "no-fault" legislation which would decrease the income of attorneys practicing in the negligence field. It is expected that this will become more pronounced in the future.

It was suggested that the contingent fee arrangment that lawyers now have unduly influences the costs of premiums by encouraging more actions and discouraging settlements.

The American Medical Association estimated that in 1971 13 percent of the nation's physicians would have had malpractice suits filed against them. Employers Mutual Insurance Company of Wausau has stated that the average annual rate for all doctors in New York State as of July 1, 1971 is $1,811 for limits of $500,000/$1,500,000. They added that the highest rate for the same coverage for a doctor who has not been surcharged for poor experience is $6,797, and that the highest rate for a doctor who has been surcharged for bad experience is over $23,000. A Hospital Association of New York State survey showed that their professional liability coverage per bed increased from $131 in 1969, to $220 in 1970, with proportionate increases assigned to outpatient visits. It is apparent that neither the doctor nor the hospital can absorb these gigantic increases. It is the patient who pays.

Nuisance and unfounded claims have a direct bearing on cost of premiums. I have proposed legislation directed at this problem which, on the motion of a defendant, would require the plaintiff to file a "good faith" bond to cover costs in the event the action is dismissed or held in favor of the defendant.

We have heard before that defensive medicine is practiced because many doctors fear malpractice suits. Patients are often overreferred to specialists; x-rays and diagnostic tests are overused; patients are often hospitalized longer than necessary; physicians may refuse emergency room duty—this all relates to the fear of malpractice as an attack upon professional competency and reputation and the fear of catastrophic financial loss.

New York State governmental agencies, quite surprisingly, lack accurate statistics regarding malpractice cases. There is no feedback of data and no mandate for reporting of vital information. In New York State three different departments are concerned with the problem—the Department of Health, the Department of Education, which rules on the licensing and reregistration of physicians, and the Department of Insurance, which regulates all insurance companies licensed to do business in our State. Yet the lack of coordination and statistical information makes it impossible for any of these to really take hold of the problem.

I have drafted and introduced a bill amending the New York State Insurance Law which would require each casualty company engaged in issuing professional medical malpractice insurance in this State, to file on a semiannual basis, with the Insurance Department a report of all claims for medical malpractice made against any of its insurees. This report would include all pertinent data relating to the claim; the amount of reserve established for the claim and at the conclusion of the claim, the manner of disposition.

We feel that having this data available in a central location will prove extremely helpful in seeking answers to many of our questions. It will certainly show us whether or not patterns are established in medical malpractice as to geographical areas of the state; age groups of physicians; disciplines of medicine usually involved in claims; social and economic groups instituting claims; and information for rate setting.

Anyone who has been actively engaged in the malpractice question quickly recognizes the maze and complexities of the issue. As a Senate Committee of the New York State Legislature our efforts are directed to perfecting a viable program of corrective measures. We have not been alone in our work by any means. There is some excellent work being done by other groups. Judge Harold Stevens' efforts in New York County through the establishment of an interprofessional arbitration panel have produced some gratifying effects. With due respect to the work of this arbitration panel, the vast number of cases being sued makes it impossible for the panel to service more than the tip of the iceberg.

I applaud and encourage the work that Judge Stevens and the members of his panel, along with others, are performing. There is, perhaps, a root problem permeating the entire field. Although my Committee has not yet concentrated on the question, we intend to examine the historical concept of negligence and award for negligence as it relates to malpractice. Should we have a no-fault principal as is being suggested for automobile liability claims? Should different degrees of injury give rise to different manners of compensation?

It is incumbent that we do all in our power to help alleviate this serious situation. We must work together harmoniously, not for the benefit of the medical profession; not for the benefit of the lawyers; not for the benefit of the insurance industry; but for the welfare of the patient.

I offer to the Chairman and members of the Secretary's Commission our full cooperation. All the resources of our Committee are at your disposal and I would hope that you will feel free to use them at your discretion.

Recommendations of New York State Special Advisory Panel on Medical Malpractice

LISTED BELOW are the recommendations of the Special Advisory Panel on Medical Malpractice contained in its report to the Governor and Legislature, January, 1976.

RECOMMENDATION No. 1

Inasmuch as the present tort law/liability insurance system for medical malpractice will eventually break down and costs have and will continue to rise to unacceptable levels, fundamental reform of the present tort law/liability insurance system should be undertaken. While the Panel does not recommend a specific compensation plan, the overriding concern should be to create a system of compensation for adverse medical outcomes resulting from medical treatment, whether or not caused by negligence. Such a system should be coordinated with other compensation systems and should limit compensation to the bona fide needs of patients.

At the same time it is imperative that we consider new ways to be sure that proper care has been rendered. The citizens of New York have a right to be assured by the State that the risk of medical injury is kept to a minimum. This companion effort will require strengthening quality controls over medical practice through a variety of measures, including disciplinary measures for substandard practice, vigorous controls over hospital staff privileges, and limitations of physician practice to areas of proven competence as demonstrated by continuing education and relicensure, if needed.

To carry this work forward, the Governor should appoint a Task Force with the charge, after proper study, to propose (1) a specific system for the consideration of the Legislature, and (2) a comprehensive program, in-

cluding proposed legislation, aimed at the prevention of medical injury and
at proper professional discipline.

The Task Force will require a period of extensive study and discussion. It should submit an interim report within one year after its appointment
and a final report with its proposals a year later. Any new system will take a
number of years to develop, and extensive public discussion will be required.
Precise definition of the compensable event will be a major consideration, especially if frivolous, minor, and unwarranted claims are to be avoided. Many
questions of administration, method and level of awards, and financing must
be examined.

To assist the Task Force in its work on injury prevention, the Health
Planning Commission should immediately launch the studies necessary to establish the extent and nature of medical injury in the health care system.
Meanwhile, the Department of Health, Department of Insurance, and the
Board of Regents should employ greater imagination and energy in the use of
their existing regulatory, safety and licensing authorities. It should be required that every health facility have an identifiable and operating injury
prevention program. Before the Task Force gets underway, a number of
other steps should be taken to up-grade the quality of medical care. The
Panel, therefore, makes a number of recommendations for immediate action
in the field of injury prevention.

RECOMMENDATION No. 2

There is no reason why all phases of medical education—undergraduate,
postgraduate, and continuing—should not be actively involved in efforts at
injury prevention. Encourage the Associated Medical Schools of New York to
be the focus for development of a medical education effort on the subject of
medical malpractice.

RECOMMENDATION No. 3

The present authority of the Medical Liability Mutual Insurance Company
(MLMIC) and the Medical Malpractice Insurance Association (MMIA) to take
account of the competence of experience of physicians needs strengthening.
Accordingly: Permit by statute the denial or cancellation of coverage of incompetent physicians by the MLMIC and MMIA, subject to authorization of
the Commissioner of Health in accordance with regulations (including ap-
peals and other procedural safeguards) jointly issued by the Commissioner of
Health and Superintendent of Insurance.

RECOMMENDATION No. 4

Require by statute second opinions or other measures to verify the need for elective surgery, if the surgery is to be compensated by third party reimbursement. Whenever such verification is required, both the initial opinion and the verification should be subject to third party reimbursement.

Reviews conducted or certified by PSRO's should be fully funded and paid for by insurers, fiscal intermediaries, and State agencies. In addition, on-site (hospital) surveys and reviews by agencies other than PSRO should be held to the minimum necessary to verify the efficacy of PSRO reviews. The Panel, therefore, recommends:

RECOMMENDATION No. 5

Strengthen the program for Professional Standards Review Organizations by providing in statute immunity to PSRO's and physician reviewers.

RECOMMENDATION No. 6

Explore through appropriate agencies ways to expand PSRO review to cover all patient care services, including those paid by private insurers.

RECOMMENDATION No. 7

Promptly issue Health Department regulations requiring reporting of cancellation or restriction of hospital privileges to physicians for reasons related to professional competence and of all malpractice claims to the Board for Professional Medical Conduct.

Some Tort law and other changes are necessary in order to prevent the imminent breakdown of the system, therefore, the Panel further recommends:

RECOMMENDATION No. 8

While the Panel sees no need to continue the duplication of payments for injury found in the present system, it recognized that adjustments should be made for premiums paid by successful claimants themselves for the period in which benefits were received. Increase costs of future insurability also need to be recognized.

Provide by statute for dollar-for-dollar offset for amounts from collateral sources with appropriate adjustments for premiums paid by the plaintiff himself.

RECOMMENDATION No. 9

Provide by statute for a limit of $100,000 on damages attributable to pain and suffering.

RECOMMENDATION No. 10

Amend Civil Procedure Law and Rules to require itemized awards.

RECOMMENDATION No. 11

Authorize by statute structured awards—including devices such as periodic payments, thrust arrangements, and guarantees of future medical services— in cases where future damages in excess of $50,000 are granted.

RECOMMENDATION No. 12

By Judicial rule, or by statute if necessary, modify and adopt Statewide the existing Schedule A as the exclusive contingent fee schedule for malpractice actions, to provide as follows: 40% of the first $25,000 recovered; 25% of the next $75,000 recovered; 15% of any recovery beyond $100,000. Keep the existing provision, which permits a court to grant a fee greater than the scale, on a showing of "extraordinary circumstances."

RECOMMENDATION No. 13

Enact legislation to prohibit the use of the ad damnum clause in medical malpractice cases.

RECOMMENDATION No. 14

Encourage the pilot project in voluntary arbitration of the Medical Society of the State of New York and the Hospital Association of New York State as an innovative experiment in new procedures for prompt and fair disposition of malpractice claims.

RECOMMENDATION No. 15

Request third party payers to revise their reimbursement practices so as to encourage self-insurance by hospitals and other institutional health care providers. The Insurance Department, the Health Department, and the Hospital Association of New York State should actively explore the utility of "claims-made" policies for hospitals.

RECOMMENDATION No. 16

Strengthen the authority of the Superintendent of Insurance for supervision of the Medical Malpractice Insurance Association.

RECOMMENDATION No. 17

With respect to data on malpractice, the Panel recommends: The Insurance and Health Departments should develop and keep current a system for reporting injury, claims, and cost data, and should accelerate their study of closed and open claims. Insurance companies should be required to comply promptly with the reporting requirements of Chapter 109. The Health Planning Commission should accelerate its efforts to secure medical injury data from the new malpractice reporting system, and all reporting systems for medical malpractice should be tied to licensing and disciplinary boards.

NOTE

The Panel notes that many proposals for change have been offered for its consideration and review. For a number of reasons . . . the Panel has not included these in its recommendations. Among the many suggested proposals were that a statutory definition of malpractice be developed, that there be further changes in the statute of limitations, in the doctrines of informed consent and res ipsa loquitur, and in rules pertaining to expert witnesses, and that mandatory binding arbitration be endorsed.

···ᓴ Appendix G ᓱ···

Recommendations of the California Citizens' Commission on Tort Reform Concerning Professional Liability

Establishing Criteria for those Professional Associations that Wish to Have their Standards of Practice Recognized in the Law

In preference to any move to establish government standard-setting mechanisms, a statute should be enacted permitting those professional associations that elect to qualify as establishers of accepted management processes and standards of professional accountability that have standing in Court to achieve this status by taking the following steps:

—Show evidence that the association is a non-profit organization which includes a substantial proportion of active practitioners of the profession in question, and has appointed a non-trivial number of public members to its governing board.

—Demonstrate the existence within the association of a formal process for developing professional standards, for revising them, for monitoring actual compliance of members, and for disciplining violators with meaningful penalties.

—Establish proof of the willingness and financial capacity to bear at least 25% of the dollar value of damages levied upon any member as a result of a malpractice action.

Any member of an association that elected to apply for this status, was certified by a designated source of State authority, and proceeded to

183

establish such standards, could cite his/her compliance with the standard as creating a rebuttable presumption that he/she had not engaged in malpractice with respect to any question that hinged upon application of the standard. Professional associations which did not elect to apply for this status would neither gain nor lose legitimacy by their choice. The Commission recognizes that professions concerned with the health and care of the human body are likely to have greatest difficulty in making effective use of this type of procedure.

Exploring Optional Automatic Payment Requirements for Some Varieties of Medical Injury

The Legislature should establish the mechanism necessary to develop and experiment with a program for compensation of victims of medical injury which embodies the following basic principles:

—Determination, by an impartial screening panel made up of people skilled in both medicine and the law, of whether a patient had experienced a Potentially Compensable Event (a finding which would *not* establish that malpractice or any other type of misconduct had occurred, only that events had proceeded in a way different from what could reasonably be expected from the patient's original problem).

—An option for the patient, after the Event, to choose whether to be compensated from a pre-set schedule of compensation benefits for various types of injuries (similar in form to the schedules in use in Workers' Compensation, in Medicare, and elsewhere), or to proceed with a tort action. The choice of one option would exclude the other, but again the choice would be made after the patient knew that he/she had suffered the Event.

—A source of finance which spreads the cost of the program as equitably as possible among users of the health care system.

Requiring Regular State Review of the Self-Disciplinary Processes Used by the Principal Professions

The Legislature should require that a detailed review be conducted at least every five years of the aggregate results of the self-disciplinary processes in each of the principal professions. The results of these reviews should be given full public disclosure.

Limiting the Third-Party Liability of Professionals to Persons who Can be Identified in Terms of General Classes

A statute should be enacted limiting a professional's liability to parties other than his/her client/patient to classes of persons who can be described in general terms.

Discouraging Concealment of Malpractice

A statute should be enacted providing that where it can be shown that a professional engaged in knowing concealment of malpractice, he/she shall be required to pay the plaintiff a surcharge of $50,000 in addition to the award.

Source: "Righting the Liability Balance," Summary of the Report of the California Citizens' Commission on Tort Reform, September 1977, pp. 15–16.

·◦[Appendix H]◦·

Highlights and Major Conclusions
of the
American Bar Association Commission
on Medical Professional Liability

THE FOLLOWING are the Commission's major conclusions and observations as a result of its work over the past two years:

1. *The underlying causes of the medical malpractice crisis of 1974–1976 were complex and involved many aspects of the health-care and tort-insurance systems.* It follows, therefore, that there are no villains against which all the blame can be assessed, and that there are no panaceas.

2. *The efforts by interest groups and state officials over the past two years, while vital in stabilizing the situation and averting interruptions in the delivery of health care services, will not solve the underlying problems.* Most of the changes in tort law and procedures are not aimed at the frequency and severity of claims; those that are will either encounter constitutional difficulties or be of inadequate effect on insurance pricing to be viewed as a "solution." . . . While the Commission has made nineteen particular recommendations concerning tort law and procedure, . . . and urges that these modifications be adopted by state legislatures, its suggestions are made in the above context. Other changes which have been suggested or enacted, such as statutory authority for arbitration or pre-trial review panels, the establishment of joint underwriting associations and improvements in medical discipline, likewise do not reach the problems in health care and the liability system which must be attacked if a reasonably permanent solution is to be attained.

3. *Even though it is clearly deficient in operation, the liability system is conceptually correct as applied to medical claims and should not be abandoned in favor of an absolute liability or social compensation system unless*

187

research clearly indicates that an adequate liability system is impossible to attain. . . .

4. *If real progress is to be made in solving the underlying problems, a variety of efforts must be undertaken to refine intermediate and long-term options and to test out various approaches.* Much of this Report deals with ongoing, contemplated or recommended work which is necessary, in the Commission's opinion, if the underlying problems are to be met. The concluding chapters of the Report summarize the particular studies and experiments the Commission believes important. However, the most critical are:

——the designated compensable event project, to be undertaken by the Commission in cooperation with medical specialty societies and the insurance industry. . . .

——the development of an effective methodology for reducing the number of medically caused injuries. The Commission hopes that this fundamental work will continue to be led by the American Hospital Association, in cooperation with national medical groups. . . .

——the development of one or more models for the resolution of medical malpractice disputes. There is a great need for clear thinking about means of dispute resolution other than the jury trial—especially arbitration, pre-trial review panels and special methods of disposing of small claims. In any study, it is important to tie dispute resolution into the prevention and loss control efforts of providers and to fashion devices which are as prompt and economical as possible, particularly at the early stages. . . .

——the intensification of lawyers' disciplinary efforts with respect to unethical conduct by some lawyers such as solicitation of cases by the use of runners or hospital employees; and fee splitting. While the Commission does not know how prevalent such practices are, it knows that they exist, and disciplinary authorities should take particular pains to see that these abuses are punished. . . .

——a thorough re-examination by the insurance industry of the lessons which may be learned from the crisis and a creative attitude towards such innovations as group marketing, "channeling" of funding or liability, the use of deductibles and periodic payment settlements. . . .

5. *The emphasis in study and reform should be at the state level, but states should be supported by national organizations and the federal government.* The tools necessary for change in the medical liability system—professional societies, insurance regulation, and legislatures—are organized strongly at the state level. In the light of this fact and the variation in problems from state to state, the Commission believes that reform efforts should be at the state level, perhaps through the creation of ongoing commissions.

Nevertheless, leadership can and should be exercised at the national level, and groups working at the state level should be able to expect leadership, funding and technical assistance from national organizations and the federal government.

     6. *As a way of grappling with issues and reducing self-serving polemics, the interdisciplinary committee has a great deal to recommend it.* The Commission unanimously supports the concept of serious, sustained discussion of medical malpractice issues by persons of different backgrounds and training. The process is not easy, but priorities do begin to come into focus. As groups at the state or national level consider how best to structure reform efforts, whether in the medical liability field or more broadly with respect to tort reform, the Commission urges that the interdisciplinary model be sympathetically considered.*

     Finally, the Commission points out that in a very basic way, the medical malpractice crisis has a great deal to do with relationships between patients and providers. . . . Physicians have an obligation to understand their patients' needs better and to explain medically-indicated tests or procedures thoroughly. Patients must understand the limitations of modern medicine (however impressive its accomplishments), and they must cooperate in following instructions. The doctor-patient relationship is not the whole key to improvement; there are many other very important aspects involving lawyers, the tort system, insurance, and the courts. But changes in that relationship, which has sometimes verged on the adversarial in recent years, could have significant catalytic effect on medical practice and patient safety programs.

*Forty-three states created commissions of one sort or another during the height of the crisis to recommend reforms which would alleviate the crisis. Understandably, most of these groups concentrated on assuring the availability of insurance and on tort law changes. The need now is for longer-term commissions, with adequate funding and staff, to delve more deeply into the underlying problems.

Source: 1977 Report of the Commission on Medical Professional Liability, American Bar Association, October 31, 1977, Chicago, Illinois.

···◦]|[◦···

Notes

CHAPTER 1

1. Proceedings of National Conference on Medical Malpractice, March 20, 21, 1975 (Washington: USGPO, 1975) 54–690, p. 7.

2. Ibid., p. 84.

3. Memorandum to Donald E. Burns, State of California, Secretary, Business and Transportation Agency, June 2, 1975, p. 2.

4. Transcript of public hearing of New York State Select Committee on Insurance Rates, Regulation and Recodification of the Insurance Laws and the State Senate Health Committee, New York City, October 4, 1974, p. 172.

5. Ibid., p. 50.

6. Actuarial Survey of Professional Medical Liability Insurance and Defense Program of the Medical Society of the State of New York, as of June 30, 1975, p. 6.

7. Letter to the New York State Insurance Department, September 24, 1975, pp. 1–2.

8. "Argonaut and Malpractice: A Tangled Web," *Medical World News,* July 14, 1975, p. 23.

9. Proceedings of Hearing Before the Subcommittee on Labor and Public Welfare, United States Senate, December 3, 1975 (Washington: USGPO, 1975), 66–972 0, p. 266.

10. Dan R. Anderson, "Face Up to the Problems of Cost," *Best's Review,* May 1975.

11. "Medical Malpractice in Michigan, A Report to Governor William G. Milliken," Lansing, Michigan, February 18, 1975, p. 4.

12. Melvin Stark, senior vice-president of governmental affairs, American Insurance Association, Program on Medical Malpractice, National Conference of State Legislatures and the Health Policy Center of Georgetown University, Washington, D.C., May 9, 1975.

13. Philip D. Miller, Medical Malpractice Arbitration Conference, New York City, April 21, 1977.

14. Proceedings of National Conference on Medical Malpractice, 1975, p. 12.

15. Interview with New York State Senate Health Committee staff, May 18, 1977.

16. Interim Report of the Office of Auditor General of the Joint Legislative Audit Committee of the California Legislature, September 10, 1975, Appendix A, p. 1.

17. Transcript of New York State hearing on insurance rates, October 4, 1974, p. 71.

18. Memorandum to Donald E. Burns, State of California, Secretary, Business and Transportation Agency, June 2, 1975, Exhibit A and Exhibit B.

19. Answers of American Insurance Association and American Mutual Insurance Alliance to questionnaire of Senator Edward M. Kennedy, Senate Health Sub-Committee, Concerning Medical Malpractice Insurance in the United States, July 17, 1975, question 33, sheet 1.

20. Report of the Industry Advisory Committee to the National Association Of Insurance Commissioners Subcommittee on Medical Malpractice, Fort Worth, Texas, January 30, 1975, p. 13.

21. Proceedings of National Conference on Medical Malpractice, 1975, p. 12.

22. Kennedy Questionnaire, July 17, 1975, question 4, sheet 5.

23. Interim Report on Auditor General, California Legislature, 1975, pp. 8–9.

24. "Preserving a Medical Malpractice Insurance Marketplace; Problems and Remedies," Position Paper and Background, St. Paul Fire and Marine Insurance Company, St. Paul, Minn., 1975, p. 1.

25. Ibid., p. 4.

26. Kennedy Questionnaire, July 17, 1975, question 4, sheets 4 and 5.

27. "Expectations, Imperfect Markets, and Medical Malpractice Insurance," paper prepared for delivery at a conference on the Economics of Medical Malpractice, Center for Health Policy Research of the American Enterprise Institute for Public Policy Research, Washington, D.C., December 15–16, 1976.

28. Kennedy Questionnaire, question 15, sheet 1.

29. Interim report, Auditor General, California Legislature, 1975, p. 9.

30. Proceedings of National Conference on Medical Malpractice, 1975, p. 13.

31. Interim Report, Auditor General, California Legislature, 1975, p. 18.

32. Ibid., pp. 20–21.

33. Ibid., pp. 40–41.

34. Transcript of New York State hearing on insurance rates, p. 72.

35. Testimony Prepared for Special Committee on Medical Malpractice of the Kansas Legislature, July 29, 1975, p. 4.

36. "The Medical Malpractice Crisis in Insurance: How it Happened and Some Proposed Solutions," The Forum (Fall 1975), p. 80.

37. Interview with New York State Senate Health Committee staff, May 10, 1977.

38. Transcript of New York State hearing on insurance rates, pp. 190–92.

39. Interview with New York State Senate Health Committee staff, May 6, 1977.

40. Ibid., September 11, 1975.

41. Ibid., May 6, 1977.

42. "Preserving A Medical Malpractice Insurance Marketplace," St. Paul, Minn., 1975, p. 3.

43. Interview with New York State Senate Health Committee staff, May 18, 1977.

44. Ibid., May 10, 1977.

CHAPTER 2

1. Proceedings of National Conference on Medical Malpractice, 1975, p. 24.

2. *Review*, Official Publication of the Federation of American Hospitals, June/July 1975, p. 6.

3. Norman Blackman, M.D., of Brooklyn, interview with New York State Senate Health Committee staff, September 16, 1975.

4. Jeffrey O'Connell, J.D., "Bypassing Medical Malpractice Claims by Contract," American College of Surgeons, September 1975 *Bulletin*, p. 7.

5. Mark C. Kendall, "Expectations, Imperfect Markets and Medical Malpractice Insurance," paper prepared for the Economics of Medical Malpractice, Washington, D.C., December 15-16, 1976, p. 17.

6. Interview with New York State Senate Health Committee staff, May 5, 1977.

7. "Who'll be Left to Treat the Patients," *Medical Economics*, April 28, 1975, p. 141.

8. Ibid., p. 132.

9. "Kennedy Plans Hearing to Study Anti-Trust Practices in Medicine," *New York Times*, June 28, 1977, p. 19.

10. "No At Any Price," paper delivered at the opening session of a conference on "Competition in the Health Care Sector," Bureau of Economics, Federal Trade Commission, Washington, D.C., June 1, 1977, p. 5.

11. William Fitzpatrick of Syracuse, interview with New York State Senate Health Committee staff, September 15, 1975.

12. John Carter, M.D., of Albany, interview with New York State Senate Health Committee staff, September 23, 1975.

13. Letter to New York State Special Panel on Medical Malpractice, August 26, 1975, p. 2.

14. The Rand Corporation, Santa Monica, California, news release, March 2, 1977, p. 3.

15. Ibid., p. 4.

16. "Malpractice Fear Stifles Heart Care, Pioneer Says," *Albany Knickerbocker News*, October 9, 1975.

17. Interview with New York State Senate Health Committee staff, May 6, 1977.

18. Donald Fager, assistant secretary and assistant treasurer of the Medical Liability Mutual Insurance Company, New York, interview with New York State Senate Health Committee staff, May 6, 1977.

19. "A Dilemma for Doctors, Patients and the Courts," *New York Times*, April 27, 1975.

20. Proceedings of National Conference on Medical Malpractice, 1975, p. 132.

21. Adrienne Astolfi, ibid., p. 49.

22. Statement for New York State Legislature's Select Committee on Insurance Rates, Regulations and Recodification of the Insurance Law and the Senate Health Committee, January 6, 1975, New York City, p. 2.

23. Statement of the American Medical Association presented to the Subcommittee on Oversight and Investigations Committee on Interstate and Foreign Commerce, U.S. House of Representatives, May 9, 1977, p. 7.

24. Ibid., p. 9.

25. Ibid., pp. 10–11.

26. Proceedings of National Conference on Medical Malpractice, 1975, p. 3.

27. Program on Medical Malpractice, National Conference of State Legislatures and Health Policy Center of Georgetown University, Washington, D.C., May 8, 1975.

28. Ibid.

29. Ibid.

30. Statement for public hearing of New York State Legislature, Select Committee on Insurance Rates, Regulations and Recodification of the Insurance Law and the Senate Health Committee, January 6, 1975, New York City, p. 9.

31. Program on Medical Malpractice, May 8, 1975.

32. Speech prepared for delivery at Medical Malpractice Training Seminar, National Conferences of State Legislatures, Dallas, Texas, February 27, 1976, p. 1.

33. Robert C. Hicks, M.D., Transcript of New York State Legislative Hearing in New York City, October 4, 1974, p. 10.

34. Ibid.

35. Sarah Joffee, M.D., New York State Legislative Hearing, pp. 416 and 417.

36. New York State hearing on insurance, pp. 333–34.

37. John H. Carter, M.D., letter to New York State Special Advisory Panel on Medical Malpractice, August 4, 1975, p. 1.

38. Report of the Committee of Interns and Residents Ad Hoc Committee on Fair Malpractice Legislation, Mount Sinai Hospital, New York City, 1975, p. 1.

39. Interview with New York State Senate Health Committee staff, September 19, 1975.

40. "Who'll Be Left to Treat the Patients," Medical Economics, April 28, 1975, p. 137.

41. The Rand Corporation, Santa Monica, California, News Release, March 2, 1977, p. 2.

42. Ibid.

43. Physicians Crisis Committee, Court Docket Survey, July 28, 1975, Detroit, Michigan, Foreword.

44. Ibid., p. 2.

45. Transcript of public hearing of New York State Select Committee on Insurance Rates on October 4, 1974, p. 306.

46. Program on Medical Malpractice, May 8, 1975.

47. Ibid.

48. Proceedings of National Conference on Medical Malpractice, 1975, p. 115.

49. Martin A. Gruber, M.D., Transcript, New York State Hearing, pp. 358–60.

50. Norman Blackman, M.D., interview with New York State Senate Health Committee staff, September 16, 1975.

51. David S. Pomrinse, M.D., Transcript of New York State Legislative Hearing on October 4, 1974, pp. 138–39.

52. Martin A. Gruber, M.D., Transcript of New York State hearing on October 4, 1974, p. 362.

53. "Interns Seeking to Form Union," Syracuse Herald American, October 12, 1975.

54. Ibid.

55. "Malpractice Crisis Overshadows Agenda as A.M.A. Session Opens," New York Times, June 15, 1975.

CHAPTER 3

1. Preliminary Report of Assembly Select Committee on Medical Malpractice, California State Legislature, June 1974, p. 44.

2. Report of the Secretary's Commission on Medical Malpractice, January 16, 1973, Department of Health, Education and Welfare Publication No. (OS) 73–88, p. 9.

3. Proceedings of National Conference on Medical Malpractice, March 20–21, 1975, Arlington, Virginia, USGPO 54–690, p. 50.

4. Testimony before New York State Special Advisory Panel on Medical Malpractice, Albany, New York, October 27, 1975, prepared statement, p. 1.

5. Ibid., p. 2.

6. James L. Groves, American Hospital Association, Interview with New York State Senate Health Committee staff, May 9, 1977.

7. Ibid.

8. Statement at public hearing of New York State Legislature's Select Committee on Insurance and Senate Health Committee, New York City, January 6, 1975, p. 9.

9. Representative Pat Burrows, Training Seminar on the Medical Malpractice Crisis, National Conference of State Legislatures, Dallas, Texas, February 28, 1976.

10. Proceedings of National Conference on Medical Malpractice, 1975, p. 6.

11. *The Investor-Owned Hospital Review*, June/July 1975, p. 12.

12. Proceedings of New York State Senate Health Committee Hospital Advisory Council Meeting, March 11, 1976, p. 28.

13. Interview with New York State Senate Health Committee staff, May 9, 1977.

14. Sally Holloway, manager, Division of Human Resources Development, American Hospital Association, Medical Malpractice Arbitration Conference, New York City, April 22, 1977.

15. "Hospitals Cut Malpractice $ in Boston Plan," *Daily News*, March 15, 1976, p. 21.

16. Daniel F. Creasey, president, Controlled Risk Insurance Company, Ltd., Interview with New York State Senate Health Committee staff, May 10, 1977.

17. Holloway, Medical Malpractice Arbitration Conference, April 22, 1977.

18. Statement prepared for public hearing of New York State Special Advisory Panel on Medical Malpractice, New York City, October 21, 1975, p. 2.

19. Ibid., p. 1.

20. Report of Assembly Select Committee on Medical Malpractice, California State Legislature, p. 45.

21. Reprinted in Proceedings of "Continuing Medical Malpractice Insurance Crisis, Hearing Before the Subcommittee on Health of the Committee on Labor and Public Welfare, United States Senate (Washington, USGPO, 1976), p. 645.

22. Preliminary Report, Assembly Select Committee on Medical Malpractice, California State Legislature, June 1974, p. 32.

23. Ibid.

24. Ibid.

25. *Medical Malpractice, A Selected Annotated Bibliography*, MACRO Systems, Inc., Silver Spring, Maryland, April 1975, p. 43.

26. Statement of Hospital Association of New York State for Public Hearing of New York State Legislature's Select Committee on Insurance and Senate Committee on Health, January 6, 1975, New York City, pp. 2–3.

CHAPTER 4

1. "You Doctors Are Making Too Much of Malpractice," *Medical Economics*, May 28, 1973, p. 174.

2. Ibid., p. 186.

3. National Conference of State Legislatures Program on Medical Malpractice, Washington, D.C., May 8, 1975, p. 1 of prepared statement.

4. Statement on behalf of the New York State Trial Lawyers Association, Inc., to the Special Advisory Panel on Medical Malpractice, Albany, New York, October 27, 1975, p. 9 of prepared statement.

5. "Malpractice," *Perspective*, Winter/76, p. 36.

6. Anne Carpenti, letter to New York State Senate Health Committee Chairman, April 28, 1977.

7. Remarks Prepared for delivery before a conference of the Council of State Governments, Newark, Delaware, July 23, 1975, pp. 4-5.

8. "Don't Injure Patients to Save Doctors," *Newsday*, April 29, 1975.

9. National Conference of State Legislatures, 1975, pp. 1-3.

10. Ibid., pp. 5-6.

11. Transcript of public hearing of New York State Legislature's Select Committee on Insurance and Senate Health Committee, October 4, 1975, pp. 403-404.

12. National Conferences of State Legislatures, 1975, p. 8.

13. Transcript of public hearing of New York State Legislature, October 4, 1974, p. 102.

14. Statement on behalf of the New York State Trial Lawyers Association, Inc., October 27, 1975, pp. 46-47, 50.

15. Bernard Hirsch, Counsel, American Medical Association, interview with New York State Senate Health Committee staff, May 10, 1977.

16. National Conference of State Legislatures, 1975, p. 10.

17. "Effects of Screening by Consultant on Recommended Elective Surgical Procedures," *New England Journal of Medicine*, 291:1133, December 19, 1974.

18. "Some Surgeons Operate for Profit: MDs," *New York Daily News*, July 15, 1975.

19. Ibid.

20. Richard D. Lyons, "Harvard Medical Group Questions Cost and Value of Much Surgery," *The New York Times*, May 24, 1977.

21. "Report Blames Surgeons in Many Preventable Deaths," *The New York Times*, April 25, 1977, p. 23.

22. "The Malpractice Threat: A Study of Defensive Medicine," Reprinted from *Duke Law Journal* 1971 (5) 964-65.

23. Statement on behalf of the New York State Trial Lawyers Association, Inc., October 27, 1975, pp. 51-52.

24. National Conference of State Legislatures, Washington, D.C., May 8, 1975.

25. Proceedings of "Continuing Medical Malpractice Insurance Crisis," 1975, Hearing before Subcommittee on Health of the Committee on Labor and Public Welfare, United States Senate, December 3, 1975 (Washington: USGPO), 66-972 0, p. 144.

26. Transcript of public hearing of New York State Legislature, October 4, 1974, pp. 401-402.

27. News Release of the State Bar of Michigan, July 29, 1975, p. 1.

28. David W. Wilson, Medical Protective Company, Prepared Statement delivered at March 31, 1977 Public Hearing, Lansing, Michigan, Classification of Anesthesiologists, File No. 76-1004-R, p. 2.

29. News Release of the State Bar of Michigan, pp. 3-4.

30. "Medical Malpractice in Michigan," A Report to Governor William G. Milliken, February 18, 1975, p. 3.

31. Statement on behalf of the New York State Trial Lawyers Association, Inc., Albany, N.Y., October 27, 1975, pp. 15, 17-19.

32. Ibid., p. 32.

33. Letter to William J. McGill, Chairman, New York State Governor's Special Advisory Panel on Medical Malpractice, October 24, 1975, p. 1.

34. Statement on behalf of the New York State Trial Lawyers Association, p. 26.

35. Letter to William McGill, Albany, New York, October 24, 1975, p. 3.

36. Transcript of public hearing of the New York State Legislature, p. 403.

37. "Don't Injure Patients to save Doctors," Newsday, April 24, 1975.

CHAPTER 5

1. Robert C. Derbyshire, *Medical Licensure and Discipline in the United States* (Baltimore: Johns Hopkins University Press, 1969) and interview with New York State Senate Health Committee staff, January 1975.

2. Proceedings of National Conference on Medical Malpractice, 1975, p. 36.

3. Edward Siegel, M.D., interview with New York State Senate Health Committee staff, September 1975.

4. Statement submitted by the American Insurance Association to the New York State Special Advisory Panel on Medical Malpractice, New York, October 21, 1975, pp. 6-7.

5. "Doctors Lose Plea Over Monitoring," *The New York Times*, November 18, 1975.

6. Statement to the *Medical World News* Editorial Board, May 3, 1974, quoted in address by Robert E. Cartwright to the National Conference of State Legislatures, May 8, 1975, Washington, D.C., p. 7 of prepared remarks.

7. Speech to a conference of the Council of State Governments, Newark, Delaware, July 28, 1975, p. 4 of prepared remarks.

8. Lewis, Howard and Martha, *The Medical Offenders* (New York: Simon and Schuster, 1970), pp. 13-14.

9. National Conference of State Legislatures, Training Seminar on Medical Malpractice Crisis, Dallas, Texas, February 27, 1976.

10. Lewis, *The Medical Offenders*, p. 38.

11. Report of the Secretary's Commission on Medical Malpractice, Department of Health, Education and Welfare, Washington, D.C., January 16, 1973, DHEW Publication No. (OS) 73-88, p. 52.

12. Address to the National Conference of State Legislatures, Washington, D.C., May 8, 1975, p. 8. Figures provided to the New York Senate Health Committee by the American Bar Association.

13. California State Legislature's Assembly Select Committee on Medical Malpractice, Preliminary Report, June 1974, pp. 53-54.

14. Ibid., pp. 53 and 54.

15. "A Study of Malpractice Deaths Reported Without Action," *The New York Times*, October 4, 1976.

16. Letter to author, April 25, 1975.

17. "Panel Urges Cancellation of Dr. Jacobson's License," *The New York Times*, April 24, 1975.

18. Thomas J. Martin, Esquire, Interview with New York State Senate Health Committee staff, May 17, 1977.

19. Ibid.

20. Ibid.

21. Claire Spiegel, "Panel Hears Grim Tale of Two Addict Doctors," *New York Daily News*, April 22, 1977, p. 48.

22. Public Hearing of New York State Assembly Medical Practice Task Force, New York City, April 21, 1977.

23. *The New York Times*, August 19, 1975, p. 29.

24. "1 Doctor in 9 Is Sick," *Syracuse Herald Journal*, April 25, 1977.

25. "Medical Profession Acting on Addict-Doctor Problem," *New York Times*, August 31, 1975.

26. Information provided to New York State Senate Health Committee by the New York State Medical Society, September 11, 1975.

27. Statement distributed to members of the New York State Legislature by the Education Department, April 14, 1975, p. 8.

28. Data received by the New York State Senate Health Committee from Thomas V. Milana, acting director of the Division of Professional Conduct, New York State Education Department, March 24, 1975.

29. Statistics provided to the Senate Health Committee by the New York State Bar Association.

30. "Medical Malpractice in Michigan, A Report to Governor William G. Milliken," February 18, 1975, p. 9.

31. Interview with New York State Senate Health Committee staff, September, 1975.

32. T. Edward Hollander, Deputy Commissioner for Higher and Professional Education, New York State Education Department, Public Hearing on Proposed Rules Defining Unprofessional Conduct, New York State Board of Regents, Albany, New York, May 10, 1977.

33. Interview with New York State Senate Health Committee staff, September, 1975.

34. "Medical Malpractice in Michigan," 1975, p. 9.

35. Preliminary Report of the California State Legislature's Assembly Select Committee on Medical Malpractice, June, 1974, p. 56.

36. Statement of the American Medical Association Before the Subcommittee on Oversight and Investigations, Committee on Interstate and Foreign Commerce, U.S. House of Representatives, May 9, 1977, pp. 3–4.

CHAPTER 6

1. Report of the Secretary's Commission on Medical Malpractice, Department of Health, Education and Welfare, Washington, D.C., DHEW Publication No. (OS) 73–88, January 16, 1973, p. VII.

2. Transcript of public hearing held by the New York State Legislature's Select Committee on Insurance and Senate Health Committee, October 4, 1974, p. 185.

3. "We Report: President's Commission on Medical Malpractice," *Trial* 9 No. (2) (March/April 1973): 30.

4. Proceedings of National Conference on Medical Malpractice, 1975, p. 131.

5. "We Report," *Trial* 9 (2) (March/April 1973): 30.

6. Report of HEW Secretary's Commission, 1973, p. 113.

7. James Ludlam, Interview, New York State Health Committee staff, May 18, 1977.

8. Proceedings of National Conference on Medical Malpractice, 1975, p. 131.

9. Interview with New York State Senate Health Committee staff, 1975.

10. Ibid.

11. Ibid.

12. Ibid.

13. Letter to Dr. William J. McGill, chairman of the New York State Special Advisory Panel on Medical Malpractice, July 22, 1975, p. 1.

14. Interview with New York State Senate Health Committee staff, 1975.

CHAPTER 7

1. Notice of Public Hearing on Medical Malpractice, New York State Senate Health Committee, September 28, 1970.

2. New York State Senate Bills 3599-E and 10569. Chapters 146 and 657, Laws of 1974.

3. Transcript of public hearing of the New York State Legislature's Select Committee on Insurance and Senate Health Committee, October 4, 1974, p. 68.

4. State of New York Insurance Department, "Cartels vs. Competition, A Critique of Insurance Price Regulations, A Report to Governor Hugh L. Carey and the New York State Legislature," 1975, p. 77.

5. Transcript of public hearing of the New York State Legislature's Select Committee on Insurance and Senate Health Committee, October 4, 1974, p. 70.

6. Ibid., p. 201.

7. Robert Carroll, "Argonaut Head Explains Pullout," *New York Daily News*, June 17, 1975.

8. State of the State Message to the New York State Legislature, January 8, 1975, p. 15.

9. "C'Mon Out, Doc, We Need You," *New York Daily News*, March 15, 1976, p. 12.

10. Transcript of New York State Senate debate, April 29, 1975, pp. 3679, 3681-83.

11. Ibid., pp. 3709-10.

12. Ibid., pp. 3701-702.

13. Ibid., p. 3670.

14. Ibid., pp. 3706-707.

15. Ibid., pp. 3622-23, 3631.

16. "Bill Would Punish Striking MDs," *Albany, New York, Times Union,* May 28, 1975.

17. "Doctors Resuming Duties After Ending Slowdown," *New York Times,* June 11, 1975.

18. Statement to the New York State Special Advisory Panel on Medical Malpractice, October 21, 1975.

19. Memorandum of Position of New York State Bar Assocation Committee on Tort Reparations in reply to written questions of New York State Special Advisory Committee on Medical Malpractice, pp. 3-4.

20. Transcript of Senate Debate, May 1, 1976, pp. 7287-88.

21. Letter to Senate Health Committee staff, May 12, 1977.

22. Remarks delivered at Medical Malpractice Arbitration Conference, April 22, 1977, New York City.

23. "Hospital Malpractice Insurance In New York State, A Policy Analysis," by Irving J. Lewis and Sandra J. Clyman, with Jeffrey H. Weiss, Policy Studies Unit, Department of Community Health, Albert Einstein College of Medicine of Yeshiva University, March, 1977, pp. 63-65.

24. "In the Matter of Public Hearing on Claims Made Form" Medical Malpractice Insurance, Opinion and Decision, State of New York Insurance Department, p. 3.

25. Attachment to letter from Sheldon Amster, director of administration, Second Judicial Department, to State Senate Health Committee, May 19, 1977.

26. Report of Medical Malpractice Program, Third Judicial Department, January 10, 1977, p. 2.

27. Letter from Cody B. Bartlett, director of administration, Fourth Judicial Department to Senate Health Committee, May 27, 1977.

28. Remarks delivered at Medical Malpractice Arbitration Conference, April 21, 1977, New York City.

CHAPTER 8

1. James Randlett, Division of Governmental Relations, California Medical Association, interview with New York State Senate Health Committee staff, December 11, 1975.

2. "California Doctors See Brown on Malpractice Insurance Issue," *The New York Times*, December 10, 1975, p. 26.

3. Remarks delivered at Training Seminar on the Medical Malpractice Crisis, National Conference of State Legislatures, Dallas, Texas, February 27, 1976.

4. Ibid.

5. Speech delivered at Annual Meeting of National Conference of State Legislatures, Philadelphia, October 9, 1975, p. 1.

6. Ibid., p. 3.

7. Interview with New York State Senate Health Committee staff, May 11, 1977.

8. James Ludlam, interview with New York State Senate Health Committee staff, May 18, 1977.

9. "The Medical Malpractice Crisis: How One State Reacted," *The Forum*, Fall 1975, p. 66.

10. Ibid., pp. 65-66.

11. Ibid., pp. 78 and 79.

12. Remarks delivered at Program on Medical Malpractice, Washington, D.C., May 9, 1975.

13. Speech to Suffolk County Medical Society, Long Island, May 19, 1977, pp. 4, 8, of prepared remarks.

14. Remarks at meeting on Medical Malpractice Insurance conducted by the Council of State Government's Eastern Regional Committee on Human Resources and Consumer Protection, May 14, 1975, Albany, New York.

15. Ibid.

16. Speech to Suffolk County Medical Society, pp. 8 and 9.

17. Robert Sullivan, Indiana State Medical Association, letter to New York State Senate Health Committee, June 6, 1977.

18. "Malpractice Law Model for Nation," *Syracuse Herald Journal*, December 8, 1975.

19. Paul F. Abrams, letter to Health Care Providers in Pennsylvania.

20. Remarks delivered at Training Seminar on the Medical Malpractice Crisis, Dallas, Texas, February 28, 1976.

21. "A Special Update and Review on Medical Malpractice Legislation and Related Court Decisions," American Medical Association, State Health Legislation Report, Vol. 5, No. 1, May 1977.

22. "The Indiana Law," The Investor-Owned Hospital Review, June/July 1975, Vol. 8, No. 3, p. 15.

23. "A Special Update and Review on Medical Malpractice Legislation and Related Court Decisions," American Medical Association, State Health Legislation Report, Vol. 5, No. 1, May 1977.

24. Interview with New York State Senate Health Committee Staff, May 11, 1977.

25. Ibid.

26. "How Lawyers Handle Medical Malpractice Cases," Research Report Series, U.S. Department of Health, Education and Welfare, Public Health Service, Health Resources Administration, DHEW Publication No. (HRA) 76–3152, Updated, p. 43.

27. James Ludlam, "Malpractice: Funding Emerges As a Critical Issue," *Trustee*, April 1976, p. 12.

28. "Death of Young Girl Blamed on Doctors' Slowdown," *Syracuse Post Standard*, December 11, 1975.

29. "How the British Do It, Malpractice Coverage for $58 a Year," Medical World News, April 21, 1975, p. 40.

30. Transcript of public hearing conducted by the New York State Legislatures Select Committee on Insurance and the Senate Health Committee, October 4, 1974, New York City, pp. 246–49.

31. "Malpractice in Canada and Elsewhere," *Perspective*, 20 75, p. 35.

CHAPTER 9

1. Medicare Provider Reimbursement Manual Revision, Part I, HIM–15–1, No. 173, April 1977, U.S. Department of Health, Education and Welfare Social Security Administration.

2. *Malpractice Digest*, April/May 1977, St. Paul Fire and Marine Insurance Co., St. Paul, Minn., pp. 1–2.

3. Interviews with New York State Senate Health Committee Staff, May 10–11, 1977.

4. Ibid.

5. Joel Edelman and Myong Kim, "The Legal Perspective," *Trustee*, December 1976, p. 11.

6. Statement of the American Medical Association, presented by James H. Sammons, M.D., before the Subcommittee on Oversight and Investigations Committee on Interstate and Foreign Commerce, United States House of Representatives, re: "unnecessary" Surgery, May 9, 1977, pp. 4–5.

7. Frank C. Abbott, assistant commissioner for the Professions, New York State Education Department, letter to New York State Senate Health Committee, June 16, 1977.

8. Iver Peterson, "L.I. Doctor Accuses 2 in Malpractice Suit," *New York Times*, May 10, 1977, p. 35.

9. Donald J. Fager, Medical Liability Mutual Insurance Company, Medical Malpractice Arbitration Conference, New York City, April 22, 1977.

10. Interview with New York State Senate Health Committee staff, May 10, 1977.

11. Ibid.

12. Medical Malpractice Arbitration Conference, New York City, April 22, 1977.

13. Letter to New York State Senate Health Committee, June 2, 1977.

14. Medical Malpractice Arbitration Conference, New York City, April 22, 1977.

15. James H. Durkin, interview with New York State Senate Health Committee staff, May 9, 1977.

16. Proceedings of National Conference on Medical Malpractice, March 21, 1975, (Washington: USGPO) 54–690, 1975, p. 55.

17. Letter to Thomas A. Harnett, New York State Superintendent of Insurance, June 20, 1977, p. 1.

18. Letter to New York State Senate Health Committee, June 1, 1977.

19. Albert J. Lipson, "Medical Malpractice: The Response of Physicians to Premium Increases in California," Prepared for the California Post-Secondary Education Commission, Contract No. PSE–35, Rand Corporation, p. v.

20. Edward J. Peterson, Executive Vice President, Good Samaritan Hospital, letter to New York State Senate Health Committee, May 18, 1977.

21. First Interim Report on Medical Practice Problems in the State of New York, a Joint Study by the Assembly Standing Committee on Health and the Assembly Standing Committee on Insurance, May 10, 1977, p. 8.

22. Joseph Boyle, M.D., California Medical Association, interview with New York State Senate Health Committee staff, May 11, 1977.

23. Interview with New York State Senate Health Committee staff, September 12, 1975.

24. Text Prepared for Delivery at National Conference on the Causes of Popular Dissatisfaction with the Administration of Justice, St. Paul, Minnesota, April 1976, pp. 23–24.

25. National Conference of State Legislatures, Philadelphia, October 9, 1975.

26. Interview with New York State Senate Health Committee staff, May 9, 1977.

27. Statement at Public Hearing of the New York State Legislature's Select Committee on Insurance and Senate Health Committee, January 6, 1975, New York City, pp. 7–8.

28. Bernard Hirsch, counsel, American Medical Association, interview with New York State Senate Health Committee staff, May 10, 1977.

29. Interview with New York State Senate Health Committee staff, May 11, 1977.

30. Program on Medical Malpractice, National Conference of State Legislatures, Washington, D.C., May 9, 1975.

31. Interview with New York State Senate Health Committee staff, May 10, 1977.

32. Ending Insult to Injury (Urbana: University of Illinois Press, 1975), pp. 30–31.

33. Interview with New York State Senate Health Committee staff, May 17, 1977.

34. "Medical Crisis: Proposed Solutions," The Forum, Fall 1975, p. 112.

35. Richard E. Lerner, associate counsel, American Arbitration Association, regional meeting of Hospital Association of New York State and New York State Medical Society, Syracuse, New York, September 19, 1975.

·◦⟩[[⟨◦·

Index

205

MEDICAL MALPRACTICE INSURANCE

was composed in ten-point Compugraphic Mallard and leaded two points,
with display type in Mallard bold by Metricomp, Inc.;
printed on 55 lb. Warren Antique Cream,
Smythe-sewn and bound over boards in Columbia Bayside Linen
by Maple-Vail Book Manufacturing Group, Inc.,
and published by

SYRACUSE UNIVERSITY PRESS
SYRACUSE, NEW YORK 13210